TRADITIONS OF CHRISTIAN SPIRITUALITY

OUR RESTLESS HEART

TRADITIONS OF CHRISTIAN SPIRITUALITY SERIES

At the Fountain of Elijah: The Carmelite Tradition
Wilfrid McGreal O. Carm.

Brides in the Desert: The Spirituality of the Beguines
Saskia Murk-Jansen

Contemplation and Compassion: The Victorine Tradition
Steven Chase

Eyes to See, Ears to Hear: An Introduction to Ignatian Spirituality
David Lonsdale

God's Lovers in an Age of Anxiety: The Medieval English Mystics
Joan M. Nuth

Journeys on the Edges: The Celtic Tradition
Thomas O'Loughlin

Mysticism and Prophecy: The Dominican Tradition
Richard Woods OP

The Poetic Imagination: An Anglican Spiritual Tradition
L. William Countryman

Poverty and Joy: The Franciscan Tradition
William J. Short OFM

Prayer and Community: The Benedictine Tradition
Columba Stewart OSB

Standing in God's Holy Fire: The Byzantine Spiritual Tradition
John Anthony McGuckin

The Spirit of Worship: The Liturgical Tradition
Susan J. White

The Way of Simplicity: The Cistercian Tradition
Esther de Waal

OUR RESTLESS HEART

The Augustinian Tradition

THOMAS F. MARTIN OSA

SERIES EDITOR:
Philip Sheldrake

Maryknoll, New York 10545

Founded in 1970, Orbis Books endeavors to publish works that enlighten the mind, nourish the spirit, and challenge the conscience. The publishing arm of the Maryknoll Fathers & Brothers, Orbis seeks to explore the global dimensions of the Christian faith and mission, to invite dialogue with diverse cultures and religious traditions, and to serve the cause of reconciliation and peace. The books published reflect the views of their authors and do not represent the official position of the Society. To learn more about Maryknoll and Orbis Books, please visit our website at www.maryknoll.org.

First published in Great Britain in 2003 by
Darton, Longman and Todd Ltd
1 Spencer Court
140–142 Wandsworth High Street
London SW18 4JJ
Great Britain

First published in the USA in 2003 by
Orbis Books
P.O. Box 308
Maryknoll, New York 10545–0308
U.S.A.

Orbis ISBN 1–57075–474–8

Printed and bound in Great Britain.

Library of Congress Cataloging-in-Publication Data

Martin, Thomas F. (Thomas Frank), 1943–
Our restless heart : the Augustinian tradition / Thomas F. Martin.
p. cm.—(Traditions of Christian spirituality)
Includes bibliographical references (p.).
ISBN 1–57075–474–8
1. Augustine, Saint, Bishop of Hippo—Influence. I. Title. II. Series.
BR65.A9 M3652 2003
270.2′092—dc21 2002152274

CONTENTS

PREFACE TO THE SERIES

Nowadays, in the western world, there is a widespread hunger for spirituality in all its forms. This is not confined to traditional religious people let alone to regular churchgoers. The desire for resources to sustain the spiritual quest has led many people to seek wisdom in unfamiliar places. Some have turned to cultures other than their own. The fascination with Native American or Aboriginal Australian spiritualities is a case in point. Other people have been attracted by the religions of India and Tibet or the Jewish Kabbalah and Sufi mysticism. One problem is that, in comparison to other religions, Christianity is not always associated in people's minds with 'spirituality'. The exceptions are a few figures from the past who have achieved almost cult status such as Hildegard of Bingen or Meister Eckhart. This is a great pity, for Christianity East and West over two thousand years has given birth to an immense range of spiritual wisdom. Many traditions continue to be active today. Others that were forgotten are being rediscovered and reinterpreted.

It is a long time since an extended series of introductions to Christian spiritual traditions has been available in English. Given the present climate, it is an opportune moment for a new series which will help more people to be aware of the great spiritual riches available within the Christian tradition.

The overall purpose of the series is to make selected spiritual traditions available to a contemporary readership. The books seek to provide accurate and balanced historical and thematic treatments of their subjects. The authors are also conscious of the need to make connections with contemporary experience and values without being artificial or reducing a tradition to one dimension. The authors are well versed in reliable scholarship about the traditions they describe. However, their intention is that the books should be fresh in style and accessible to the general reader.

One problem that such a series inevitably faces is the word 'spirituality'. For example, it is increasingly used beyond religious circles and does not necessarily imply a faith tradition. Again, it could mean substantially different things for a Christian and a Buddhist. Within Christianity itself, the word in its modern sense is relatively recent. The reality that it stands for differs subtly in the different contexts of time and place. Historically, 'spirituality' covers a breadth of human experience and a wide range of values and practices.

No single definition of 'spirituality' has been imposed on the authors in this series. Yet, despite the breadth of the series there is a sense of a common core in the writers themselves and in the traditions they describe. All Christian spiritual traditions have their source in three things. First, while drawing on ordinary experience and even religious insights from elsewhere, Christian spiritualities are rooted in the Scriptures and particularly in the Gospels. Second, spiritual traditions are not derived from abstract theory but from attempts to live out gospel values in a positive yet critical way within specific historical and cultural contexts. Third, the experiences and insights of individuals and groups are not isolated but are related to the wider Christian tradition of beliefs, practices and community life. From a Christian perspective, spirituality is not just concerned with prayer or even with narrowly religious activities. It concerns the whole of human life, viewed in terms of a conscious relationship with God, in Jesus Christ, through the indwelling of the Holy Spirit and within a community of believers.

The series as a whole includes traditions that probably would not have appeared twenty years ago. The authors themselves have been encouraged to challenge, where appropriate, inaccurate assumptions about their particular tradition. While conscious of their own biases, authors have none the less sought to correct the imbalances of the past. Previous understandings of what is mainstream or 'orthodox' sometimes need to be questioned. People or practices that became marginal demand to be re-examined. Studies of spirituality in the past frequently underestimated or ignored the role of women. Sometimes the treatments of spiritual traditions were culturally one-sided because they were written from an uncritical Western European or North Atlantic perspective.

However, any series is necessarily selective. It cannot hope to do full justice to the extraordinary variety of Christian spiritual traditions. The principles of selection are inevitably open to question. I hope that an appropriate balance has been maintained between a sense of the likely readership on the one hand and the dangers of narrowness on the other. In the end, choices had to be made and the result is inevitably weighted in favour of traditions that have achieved 'classic' status or which seem to capture the contemporary imagination. Within these limits, I trust that the series will offer a reasonably balanced account of what the Christian spiritual tradition has to offer.

As editor of the series I would like to thank all the authors who agreed to contribute and for the stimulating conversations and correspondence that sometimes resulted. I am especially grateful for the high quality of their work which made my task so much easier. Editing such a series is a complex undertaking. I have worked closely throughout with the editorial team of Darton, Longman and Todd and Robert Ellsberg of Orbis Books. I am immensely grateful to them for their friendly support and judicious advice. Without them this series would never have come together.

PHILIP SHELDRAKE
Sarum College, Salisbury

ABBREVIATIONS

AugAges	*Augustine Through the Ages: An Encyclopedia*
civ.	*De ciuitate dei libri uiginti duo*, City of God
conf.	*Confessiones*, Confessions
corrept.	*De correptione et gratia liber unus*, On Admonition and Grace
doct. chr.	*De doctrina Christiana libri quattuor*, On Christian Doctrine
en. Ps.	*Enarrationes in Psalmos*, Explanation of the Psalms
ep. Io. tr.	*In epistulam Iohannis ad Parthos tractatus decem*, Tractates on the First Letter of John
ep.	*Epistula*, Letter(s)
Io. eu. tr.	*In Iohannis euangelium tractatus*, Tractates on the Gospel of John
praed. sanct.	*De praedestinatione sanctorum*, On the Predestination of the Saints
retr.	*Retractationes*, Retractations
s., ss.	*Sermo, sermones*, Sermon(s)
sol.	*Soliloquiorum libri duo*, The Soliloquies
trin.	*De trinitate libri quindecim*, The Trinity
virg.	*De sancta virginitate liber unus*, On Holy Virginity
WSA	The Works of Saint Augustine, A Translation for the 21st Century (1990–)

INTRODUCTION

Augustine of Hippo, that man of restless heart, has profoundly shaped Western Christianity. As God-seeker, philosopher, convert, contemplative monk, literary artist, busy bishop, theologian and polemicist, he sought to make sense of himself and humanity before God – and in so doing left behind a spiritual and literary heritage that thoughtfully, eloquently and often provocatively recounts that effort. The restless heart of Augustine prompted a searching, a commitment to truth and love, an unrelenting desire to engage the mystery of God that unfolded before him, both overwhelming and beckoning him.

No one can deny his formative role in shaping the spirituality of Western Christianity, though for some it is a cause for concern. It is, perhaps, impossible to remain indifferent before Augustine. Such reactions would probably not surprise him, this multifaceted Late Antique man – for even in his lifetime his theological positions and his spiritual vision were not without critics. This volume is intended to be an excursion into the rich history that is the spiritual tradition identified with St Augustine. Given the volume of his writings, the enormous response they have generated, the crowded field of those who label themselves or are labelled 'Augustinians', as well as the ample debates they too have prompted, this excursion can only claim to be a brief but representative entry into a tradition that is vast, complicated, and as much discussed today as it was in Augustine's time.

This study begins with Augustine himself and then traces the legacy of his spiritual vision as it is taken up by representative thinkers and seekers through the centuries. The Belgian

Augustinian scholar T. van Bavel has referred to Christian spirituality as a 'window upon the gospel' – a real yet necessarily limited way of looking at the Jesus Christ who is revealed there. The gospel landscape, he suggests, is as vast as it is profound; thus 'many windows' are needed to gaze upon this unified yet infinite panorama. The 'Augustinian tradition' is one such window, the product of Augustine of Hippo's experience and understanding of God, how this experience and understanding continued and continues to be read, understood and lived. This vision undoubtedly reflects all that is unique about Augustine of Hippo, this ancient man. Here, in this imposing figure, it seems that one ought to find the locus of Augustinian spirituality. Yet, when one looks to him, at least if the looking is serious and critical, it is clear that Augustine is never pointing to himself but to the Other: the Word made flesh, the Word of the Father who speaks love, as God's Spirit of love is poured forth into human hearts (Romans 5:5, the basis of this statement, was a favourite of his); the Word who judges us by saying 'I was hungry and you gave me no food' (Matthew 25:31–46 was never far from Augustine's heart or discourse). Augustine saw himself as a pilgrim and seeker, called, stimulated and guided by the Word. His intent was to invite others to make the journey and thus we are meant to share with him the adventures, the joys, the sorrows, the learnings, the demands that came to him during the actual course of his spiritual journey as our own invitation and admonition to enter upon the path of Christ. Thus, to be faithful to Augustine, the story of the Augustinian tradition cannot simply be about him, but likewise about the Christ-journey he proposes for all of us.

Augustine of Hippo has left more writings than any ancient Christian author. Like so many other thinkers of those distant centuries his approach tended toward the expansive and digressive. He was nurtured by a culture that was fundamentally oral and rhetorical, where neither brevity nor linear thinking were prized virtues. In addition, many of his writings were circumstantial or polemical, often without explicit reference to the full scope of his thought. These qualities challenge us to be different kinds of readers if we wish to reach the real heart and mind of Augustine, seeking to set even brief excerpts or phrases within the larger landscape of his thought.

Each of this book's excursions into later traditions will evaluate them from a perspective firmly grounded in Augustine. The first two chapters will attempt to provide that foundation. Chapter 1 offers a synthetic view of his spiritual vision. Chapter 2 presents Augustine's monastic vision, chiefly as expressed in the Augustinian *Rule*. Passing over many intermediate centuries, Chapter 3 will take up the Augustinian tradition in the eleventh and twelfth centuries, exploring the reading of Augustine undertaken by reforming Canons, in particular the Victorines of Paris. Chapter 4 will turn to the Mendicant reforms of the thirteenth and fourteenth centuries, with a specific consideration of the new reading of Augustine brought forward by the Hermit Friars of St Augustine, known today as the Order of St Augustine. Chapter 5 will explore the shared yet contentious readings of Augustine by Protestant and Catholic humanists and reformers, at a time when the West was seeking to revitalise its spiritual vision. Chapters 3, 4 and 5 thus deal with the question of spiritual reform and renewal, with the authority of Augustine serving as touchstone and rallying point during times of transition and spiritual turmoil. Chapter 6 will engage the 'modern' and ongoing encounter with Augustine and his spiritual vision. The modern era, understood in the broadest sense of the word, is marked by one revolution after another: the Enlightenment, industrialisation, secularisation, totalitarianism, wars great and small, the Second Vatican Council, postmodern revisionism. The name, authority and thought of Augustine reverberate throughout these periods of cultural and spiritual shifts, at least in those thinkers intrigued by the Bishop of Hippo's unique engagement with the mystery of the human condition. In the Conclusion I will both retrospectively and prospectively offer some brief comments regarding this rich and complex tradition associated with Augustine. By examining what made his spirituality so significant through these many centuries, it may be possible to understand why even today he continues to be a focal point for all those who take seriously the restlessness of the human heart, seeking, like Augustine, to make sense of its insistent summons.

One of the striking elements of the spiritual tradition associated with the name Augustine of Hippo is its intensely intellectual character. Throughout its history it has been marked by what might be called an intellectual piety, a 'thinking' spirituality, in which both philosophical and theological inquiry are decidedly spiritual practices. Augustine was a committed thinker and searcher; he took to heart Jesus' admonition in the Sermon on the Mount to ask, and seek, and knock (Matthew 7:7). 'Unless you believe you will not understand' (Isaiah 7:9, LXX) provided sure biblical ground for an approach to the Christian life that linked study, reading, dialogue and inquiry with prayer, holiness, community and love. This characteristic of Augustine may challenge many readers to rethink their assumptions about the nature and content of spirituality in general and about Augustinian spirituality in particular.

One historical fact is both certain and fascinating: in times of transition there has been an almost automatic turn to the figure and writing of Augustine, if not to follow the exact path he proposed and trod, then at least to let him help us to consider our own next steps more thoughtfully. Thus this study of the Augustinian tradition is intended not only to shed light on how ages past have sought to learn from his spiritual teaching but also to make available to the transitions of the present time the wisdom and depth of his thought and experience.

Many 'Augustinian voices' have played a part in this project and to them I am most indebted. They have saved me from many errors in this work; those that remain are my own. I have had the privilege of dialoguing with my Augustinian brothers and sisters in Asia, Australia, Africa, South America, Europe and North America – they have taught me much about

Augustine. I am most grateful to Villanova University for granting me sabbatical time and to the Collegio Santa Monica and Augustinianum in Rome for their fraternal hospitality and the setting of a learning community in which to bring this work to completion. I owe a particular word of thanks to Allan Fitzgerald OSA and Barbara Agnew CPPS for their patient reading of this manuscript and their helpful criticism. Finally, this work would not have been possible without the support of my Augustinian brothers of St Augustine Friary and Burns Hall, Villanova, Pennsylvania who bore with me during the course of this project. It is to my Augustinian brothers and sisters that I dedicate this volume.

1. THE JOURNEY: AUGUSTINE'S SPIRITUAL VISION

Augustine of Hippo's life (354–430 CE) spans a knotty yet pivotal period of early Christian history. At the time of his birth the Christian theological world was still bitterly divided over questions concerning the Council of Nicaea (325). At the time of his death, the Western Roman Empire was fast approaching political disintegration, thus bringing to a close more than a thousand years of history. This Roman world of Late Antiquity was by no means a gentle world: violence was ever at its frontiers and local political rebellion was common. Neither complacency nor tolerance were considered virtuous in this world, and this held true also for the Christian church. It is against this backdrop that a Roman landowner of modest means named Patricius and a remarkably resilient North African woman named Monnica welcomed a son whom they named Augustine, on 13 November 354. The mother's devout Catholic piety was matched by the non-Christian father's religious indifference, and in the course of his first decades the promising young boy would reflect both parents' religious stance.

We quite possibly know more about Augustine of Hippo than any ancient figure; and this knowledge equips us to see his spirituality as flowing from and inserted into this very real world. Augustine's spirituality was never a theoretical exercise but always an attempt to respond to the demand to be a Christian in the religious, cultural and political setting that was late fourth- and early fifth-century Roman Africa.

UNEXPECTED GRACE

First and foremost, Augustine was shaped by his personal history. His early upbringing was the responsibility of his devoutly Catholic mother who clearly made her faith part and parcel of his infant care and education. 'For with my mother's milk my infant heart had drunk in and still held deep down in it that name [of Christ] according to your mercy, O Lord, the name of Your Son, my Savior' (*conf.* 3.4.8).[1] Yet, despite his mother's religiosity, so taken for granted were the sins of youth, according to the practice of the day, that his baptism was deferred. Aware of his brilliance, his parents stretched their resources and looked for outside benefaction in order to see to the finest education available in Roman Africa. It is clear that they saw their own fame and security tied to the fortunes of their gifted and remarkable son. He eventually found himself at the head of his class of aspiring rhetoricians in Carthage, well grounded in the standard curriculum of the liberal arts that was the mainstay of ancient Roman education. Literature, dialectics, philosophy, oratory – with these tools Augustine was prepared for a successful career, with the hope of retiring at a reasonably young age to a life of educated leisure. In fact, Augustine will eventually put these intellectual tools to a totally unforeseen use, as pastor, spiritual guide and religious thinker.

During his training in the art of persuasion at Carthage he was himself persuaded and won over by the Manichaeans, remaining with this controversial religious group for over a decade. The Manichaeans were always talking about Christ, as Augustine tells us in his *Confessions* (3.6.10), and promised their 'hearers' a rational doctrine that was proposed as superior to his mother's 'womanish' Catholic faith. At this time, as well, he took a companion with whom he lived for thirteen years and together they were challenged to welcome an unanticipated son whom they named Adeodatus, literally 'gift of God'. But at certain key moments in his early years with the Manichaeans he began to discover that little of substance was to be found behind the complexities of their doctrines. Yet despite this disillusionment, he continued his association with them, since their often well-placed membership seemed to offer him the requisite stepping stones for future advancement. He was not disappointed, for they assisted his move from the unruly students at Carthage, to non-paying Roman students, and eventually to the chair of rhetoric in Milan, then residence of the Western Emperor. This move brought Augustine into courtly society where his ambitions for success and wealth could find appropriate satisfaction. In Milan his rhetorical duties included official public speeches on notable imperial occasions, oratory intended to dazzle leading members of the court and Milanese high society, his gateway to a secure future.

In Milan he also encountered Ambrose, the unexpected beginning of the end of a life dedicated to success and fortune:

> So I came to Milan, to the bishop and devout servant of God, Ambrose, famed among the best men of the whole world . . . All unknowing I was brought by God to him, that knowing, I should be brought by him to God. That man of God received me as a father . . . (*conf.* 5.13.23)

These and other contacts led him to conversations and books that precipitated intellectual and religious conversion. First he encountered 'the books of the Platonists' (*conf.* 7.20.26), which enabled him to intellectually conceive of 'spiritual reality' and move away from the grossly materialistic worldview of the Manichaeans. However, he not only read philosophy. He turned to Scripture and especially St Paul (*conf.* 7.21.27). These readings provoked a profoundly spiritual crisis that triggered a chain of occurrences that once and for all put Augustine into the embrace of Christ. In the *Confessions* he recounts the famous garden scene that led to his conversion:

> And suddenly I heard a voice from some nearby house, a boy's voice or a girl's voice, I do not know: but it was a sort of sing-song, repeated again and again, 'Pick it up! Read!

> Pick it up! Read!' . . . Damming back the flood of my tears I arose, interpreting the incident as quite certainly a divine command to open my book of Scripture and read the passage at which I should open . . . So I was moved to return to the place where Alypius [his closest friend and witness to the events] was sitting, for I had put down the Apostle's book there when I arose. I snatched it up, opened it, and in silence read the passage upon which my eyes fell: 'Not in dissipation and drunkenness, nor in debauchery and lewdness, nor in arguing and jealousy; but put on the Lord Jesus Christ, and make no provision for the flesh or the gratification of our desires' (Romans 13:13–14). I had no wish to read further, and no need. For in that instant, with the very ending of the sentence, it was as though a light of utter confidence shone in all my heart, and all the darkness of uncertainty vanished away. (*conf.* 8.12.29)

Augustine portrays his conversion as surprising and unrehearsed, fully God's work. Yet those familiar with the narrative of the *Confessions* are left with little doubt that the ground of his heart had long been being prepared through events, people and books for that final moment in the garden.

The subsequent events in Augustine's life repeat the experience of unanticipated and transformative grace: a journey back to Africa interrupted by civil war and the death of his mother; a return to Africa into a fledgling monastic community on his family estate, where his desire for retreat was met by sudden fame; the deaths of his son Adeodatus and his close friend Nebridius within a short span of time. But nothing was more unanticipated than the outcome of a visit to the Roman African port city of Hippo Regius. Fearing that his fame would lead him into church affairs, he deliberately avoided cities that did not have a bishop. In 391, while visiting Hippo on behalf of his developing monastic project, he was unexpectedly drafted into the priesthood. The bishop there, Valerius, was Greek speaking and was looking for a capable Latin assistant. The particular Sunday Augustine entered that church Valerius expressed that desire once again and all eyes turned to Augustine. His life was never to be the same. From 391 until his death in 430 he held in delicate balance the roles and tasks chosen by him and chosen for him: monk, priest-then-bishop, preacher and teacher, civic leader and judge, voice of the church of Africa, prominent theologian, correspondent, polemicist, but above all a man 'intent upon God'. Throughout these four decades his voice and pen would never tire trying to explore and explain that mysterious bond that unites humanity with God.

Augustine felt quite unprepared for the spiritual journey he found himself called to undertake with ordination. Perhaps the very abruptness of the call fostered the intensity that would mark his entire religious life: his unflagging attention to certain key themes and principles; an uncompromising tenacity regarding what he understood to be the rule of faith; a brilliant gift for polemics and debate. This intensity was certainly encouraged by the contentiousness that marked the church and society of his day, as well as by the fragility that conditioned so much of human life. In Augustine's world everyday journeying was precarious and its tomorrows always uncertain – little could be taken for granted. His spiritual vision is surely shaped by this world and is a product of his deliberate effort to respond evangelically to its demands.

APPROACHING AUGUSTINE

A perennial challenge for students of Augustine is both the sheer volume of his writings and the nature of those writings. The output of four decades of pastoral ministry, controversy and devotion, it is the largest collection of any ancient author. It presents a lifetime project for anyone undertaking a complete knowledge of Augustine. What makes such a study even more daunting is the fact that the vast majority of his works are situational, addressing particular problems at a particular point in history. Thus they do not represent an ordered system of thought. Furthermore, Augustine makes it clear that there was movement and development in his thinking. Late in life he will chide some of his devoted but confused admirers for not growing with him in theological understanding, even regarding his own works:

> You see clearly what my thoughts were then concerning faith and works, as I was laboring ever so much to commend the grace of God. I see that our brothers did not take the same care to make progress with me as they did to read my books. (*praed. sanct.* 4.8)

Augustine admonishes these readers to study him carefully and, in this case, to progress in thought as he did, to pay careful attention to the chronology of his works. Would he not insist on the same today?

Further, modern readers will often find themselves tested by Augustine's writing techniques, at odds with modern expectations of a certain kind of literary logic and systematisation. But what may appear to us as a rambling and digressive approach must be understood in the light of an ancient world that remained more oral than literary. It was indeed a world of great literature but even the written word was set down to be spoken out loud and heard. Thus 'readers' in the ancient world were almost always 'listeners' as well, even when reading alone. Augustine recounts in the *Confessions* his surprise at coming upon Ambrose reading silently (*conf.* 6.3.3), so strikingly different was the practice. Furthermore, an oral culture might be said to reason cumulatively rather than systematically; Walter Ong characterises orality as additive, aggregative, copious, agonistic and participatory.[2] What that means, for example, is that when one reads Augustine for any length of time, one can have the feeling of being pummelled by wave after wave of scriptural quotes, repeated words or phrases, questions asked over and over again; and sometimes all this occurs in the course of a single dense paragraph. This is not our world of communication but an oral world where repetition and redundancy are standard fare. What often holds his thought together is not systematic or thematic order but verbal and rhetorical resonance and repetition. Arguments, concepts, questions and principles are repeatedly reasserted, but these recurring themes, when taken together, reveal the centre and unity of his spiritual vision.[3] The student of Augustine can sometimes be tempted to isolate singular and often dramatic ideas from this larger configuration, the very artistry and power of a single theme repeated over and over thus misleading the incautious or inexperienced reader. This is why the study of his thought and spirituality demands a conscious effort to link exceptionally compelling and dramatically expressive ideas into his larger, often implicit and certainly intricate framework of ideas. The oral-rhetorical-polemical world of Augustine demanded an emphatic insistence upon the circumstantial and particular, and expected the reader to possess the ability to integrate it into a wider context. As will be seen in the subsequent chapters, failure to understand Augustine holistically will sometimes haunt the Augustinian tradition.

THE JOURNEY

Keeping the above in mind, I propose a foundational metaphor or image to help in understanding the spirituality of Augustine, one that holds together a host of distinctive, even seemingly contradictory affirmations. I propose that it is with the notion of 'the journey' (*peregrinatio*) that one finds a key to understanding and living Augustinian spirituality. For Augustine and his world *peregrinatio* connotes not only the actual travelling to a desired destination, but all of the preparations and concerns necessary for its accomplishment: mapping, over-nighting, provisioning, security, choice of companions and, most importantly, knowledge of the destination. 'Everyone', Augustine will insist, 'knows what the journey demands' (*en. Ps.* 42.2). Of course, he did not invent the image; it is an integral part of ancient thought from Homer's *Odyssey* to Virgil's *Aeneid*, and even to Plotinus' *Enneads*, which offers a map for the soul's journey to the One.[4] It is a foundational biblical theme from Abram's call to go forth (Genesis 12:1), to the Psalms of Ascent,[5] and it resounds in Jesus' cry: 'I am the way' (John 14:6). In Augustine's world everyone knew that it was sometimes necessary to leave the security of city walls and fortified households, and traverse dangerous and unpredictable terrain, to arrive at a safe destination. Safe arrival could never be taken for granted: one might lose the way, be overtaken by brigands, encounter storms. In the *Confessions* Augustine recounts how Monnica's sea voyage from Africa to Italy to join her son in Milan nearly met with shipwreck (6.1.1). His biographer Possidius notes how radical Donatists had once planned to ambush him in the course of a journey, but his party made a wrong turn and so escaped with their lives.[6] Much of what we today understand to be encompassed by the term 'spirituality' can be summed up by the tension and energy, risk and excitement, reluctance and expectation of Augustine's notion of the journey (*peregrinatio*).

> 'Alas, that I am a stranger in a distant land.' I have gone far from you, my pilgrimage has become long in duration. I have not yet come to that homeland where I will not be overcome by some misfortune; I have not yet arrived in that community of Angels where I need fear no scandal. Why am I not there? 'Alas, that I am a stranger in a distant land.' To sojourn away from home is a pilgrimage: one who is 'in passage' is dwelling in a foreign land, not at home . . . (*en. Ps.* 119.6)

In drawing upon this profoundly resonant ancient image, Augustine offers a compelling vision of the Christian life – and its destination. His world knew that the journey was always unpredictable and arduous, but this very fact only served to increase longing for safe homecoming: 'there is only one sweet homeland, one true homeland, everything else for us is pilgrimage (*peregrinatio*)' (*en. Ps.* 61.7). Augustine will allow neither himself nor his listeners to forget the journey, unceasingly chiding all to hold the course, to remember they are pilgrims, members of a community of journeyers. What marks Augustine's spiritual vision is that he came to know the journey: where he was going, how he was going to get there, where constantly to direct his gaze, and that it was a journey to be shared. In what follows we will see how rich and demanding the metaphor is, experientially, biblically and theologically, and how it imbues Augustine's thought with a spirit of searching, a dynamism and, inevitably, a holy but often disturbing tension.[7] Augustine's heart was ever on a restless journey – we will need to see if the Augustinian tradition remained and remains true to this foundational insight and perspective.

THE CHRIST-JOURNEY

Perhaps the best-known incident in the life of Augustine, recorded in the already-cited final paragraphs of Book Eight of his *Confessions*, is his 'conversion'.[8] It began with a bout of tears that sent him to a remote corner of the garden of his house in Milan. His dear friend and heart-brother Alypius (*conf.* 9.4.7), present at a discreet distance, was a witness to the event. His cries and laments directed to God were interrupted by a strange and unaccustomed voice wafting from a nearby house: 'Pick it up! Read! Pick it up! Read! – *Tolle! Lege! Tolle! Lege!*' 8.12.29). It sounded like the game-chant of children at play but Augustine cannot ever remember hearing such a rhyme. He took it, in imitation of the *Life of Antony*, as God's voice addressed specifically to him and hurried back to the place where he had left his dear friend Alypius as well as a copy of the Scriptures, in fact, a book of St Paul's letters. The 'Pick it up! Read!' became 'Read Paul!' as he commits himself to take to heart the first passage he lights upon. It is Romans 13:13–14:

> So I was moved to return to the place where Alypius was sitting, for I had put down the Apostle's book there when I arose. I snatched it up, opened it, and in silence read

> the passage upon which my eyes fell: 'Not in dissipation and drunkenness, nor in debauchery and lewdness, nor in arguing and jealousy; but put on the Lord Jesus Christ, and make no provision for the flesh or the gratification of our desires.' (*conf.* 8.12.29)

It is striking and even dismaying to note how often commentators emphasise the asceticism of the first and closing words of the Pauline passage from Romans and completely ignore its central call: 'Put on the Lord Jesus Christ.' There was much more than world-fleeing under way for Augustine. In fact, he was not fleeing as much as he was finding, or, even more correctly, being found, by that 'light of utter confidence' that he suddenly experienced 'penetrating his heart' (*quasi luce securitatis infusa cordi meo*). While his 'putting on the Lord Jesus Christ' was certainly a final decision to be baptised, it also meant letting Jesus Christ become the driving love, the stable centre, the total preoccupation of his life. 'Put on the Lord Jesus Christ' can indeed be looked upon as the absolute statement of the nature of Augustine's spiritual journey, but because of this it will also be seen as the key to understanding Augustine himself. To know Augustine is above all to recognise that Jesus Christ is at the foundation and core of all he did and wrote.[9]

Students of Augustine's spirituality have tended to ignore his theology of Christ, often for the simple reason that his undoubtedly monumental trinitarian efforts have for so long held their primary attention. Recent scholarship, however, has begun to insist upon the central place that the mystery of Christ plays in his thought.[10] It is stated boldly by one commentator to be 'the condition, the author and the method of all his thinking'. 'Christ is not so much an object of his speculation, but the source and method for [Augustine's] philosophical and theological thinking.'[11] Why has this gone so unnoticed? It is so pervasive and constitutive of Augustine, as suggested by the comments just quoted, that it can easily go unnoticed. The neglect is also a by-product of a scholarship that tended to read Augustine selectively. Fortunately, a renewed interest in Augustine's preaching and the awareness that the homily is as much a part of Augustine's thought as are his more formal theological writings is welcome because that is where the centrality of Christ is often most clear. There is room here for much more explanation and commentary but it is best to look more closely now at Augustine's Christ.

CHRIST THE WAY AND THE HOMELAND

Augustine's christological intent, and the key to the spirituality he offers, was a lifelong theological-spiritual project to place the person, identity, mission and presence of Jesus Christ – 'human divinity and divine humanity – *humana divinitas et divina humanitas Christi*' (*s.* 47.21) at the centre of the spiritual consciousness, religious imagination and daily living of his Christian community. He did this with theological determination as well as bold artistic imagination, seeking to do justice to both the demands of orthodoxy[12] and the incomprehensibility of the mystery. The results are a strikingly new sense of self, community, culture and cosmos, all anchored in an unrelenting affirmation of 'the one mediator between God and humanity, Jesus Christ himself human' (1 Timothy 2:5).[13] Thus all of Augustine's efforts must be understood to point towards Christ: 'You're not yet home (*in patria*), you're still on the way (*in via*) . . . Where are we going? To Christ. How do we get there? Through Christ (*Quo imus? Ad Christum. Qua imus? Per Christum*)' (*en. Ps.* 123.2). Christ is the only way (*via*), as well as the final and absolute destination or true homeland (*patria*) for humanity.[14] While such an insistence upon the centrality of Christ might be expected of any Christian thinker, in Augustine's case, and especially considering his precise historical and theological moment, one can say without exaggeration that no previous Christian thinker had sought with such comprehensiveness and rigour to place every aspect of human life and created reality under a deliberately christological lens: from heart, to human body, to relationships, to politics, to culture and beyond. And yet all the while he never allows us to lose sight of the profound trinitarian dimensions of this affirmation.[15] Jesus the Christ reveals the Trinity and the Trinity is once and for all manifested in the life and teaching of Jesus Christ.

One way to appreciate Augustine's understanding of Christ as *via* and *patria* is to consider some of his preferred titles or names that express for him who Christ is and what he accomplishes. Found abundantly throughout his writing, they are not only statements of faith but equally calls to respond in faith. Four will be considered here: Christ the Word, Christ the healer, the poor Christ and the whole Christ. He draws them from the Scriptures and through them offers a vision of Jesus Christ that is almost overwhelming, yet intimately personal and relational. These titles reveal a multifaceted and intimate companion who calls us to the journey, journeys with us, makes the very journey possible, and is, as well, its joyful and secure destination.

Christ the Word (*Christus Verbum*)

Christ the Word is a title which is at the centre of much of Augustine's christological explorations. Taken above all from the Johannine prologue, it is, for Augustine, a cornerstone affirmation of the full divinity and complete humanity of Jesus Christ. Given his training and immersion in the world of rhetoric – Augustine pejoratively describes himself as a 'word vendor' (*conf.* 9.2.2) – it is not surprising that he seizes upon the richness and possibility of all that is involved in the notion of the Word. In his preaching, in the setting of the Liturgy, he found a privileged occasion for inviting the faithful into the mystery of the Word: its divine reality, its discursive power, its symbolic potential and its mysterious elusiveness. John's gospel and its theology of the Word (the only gospel that merited a full commentary by Augustine) gave him an inexhaustible narrative that could speak to the depths of the human heart. The very obscurity of the Johannine narrative, when compared with the Synoptics, epitomised the depth of the mystery of the Word made flesh. The striking image of John at the Last Supper resting his head upon the bosom of Jesus (*super pectus Domini*) moved him deeply: here Augustine recognised both Christian identity and task. He notes, for example, how we are to 'press our own hearts against the Word – *usque ad Verbum cor habere*' (*en. Ps.* 21.II.19). The Word is never mere letters, syllables and sounds dispensed for human ears to receive. Christ speaks to our heart and thus our human condition, to the deepest longings and desires that are God-placed within. Augustine tells God in the *Confessions*: 'You shattered my heart with your word – *percussisti cor meum verbo tuo*' (*conf.* 10.6.8) – not destruction but new creation. 'You pierced our heart with your love, and we bore your piercing words in our depths – *sagittaveras tu cor nostrum caritate tua, et gestabamus verba tua transfixa visceribus* . . .' (*conf.* 9.2.3) – not invasive but transformative presence. Christ the Word speaks the Father's love and in that very speaking reorientates all discourse, even one's private inner dialogue – in his *Confessions* Augustine offers a model for such transformation.

Christ the Healer: *Christus Medicus*

Words that touch, delight and transfigure the human heart suggest a second powerful christological title for Augustine: Christ the healer (understood as comprehensively as possible: physician, surgeon, therapist, pharmacologist, specialist . . .). It is in the astonishing healing power of *Christus medicus* that Augustine proposes we encounter the divinity of Christ in a deeply personal way. Augustine suffered from poor health throughout his life. This may explain why he always seemed to be intensely interested in and fascinated by the art and practice of medicine, and why he was well versed in the latest medical theory and practice of his day. Speaking of health matters also seemed to touch a very deep and responsive chord within the hearts of his listeners. It was a world exposed to the worst kind of medical quackery,[16] where, even at its best, treatment seemed more torment than assistance. One of Augustine's favourite comments about faith is: 'You're willing to trust these doctors and you're unwilling to trust God?'

> How much doctors do against the will of their patients, and yet they are not doing it against their health. The doctor sometimes makes a mistake, God never. So if you entrust yourself to a doctor who can make mistakes sometimes, you are entrusting yourself to human treatment – and not just for dressing which is soothing, or some bandaging which doesn't hurt you, but very often it is for him to burn, to cut, to remove a limb that was born with you and for you, that you entrust yourself to him. You don't say, 'What if he has it all wrong and I will be minus one finger!' You allow him to cut, in case it should infect your whole body. And you won't allow God to operate upon you, to amputate some of your wealth [he is preaching here about trusting God in the face of financial loss!]? (*s.* 15A.8)

The healing power, programme and practice of Christ the physician are repeatedly brought before Augustine's listeners as he lays out for them what he calls God's 'medicinal saving economy – *dispensatio medicinalis*' (*Io. eu. tr.* 36.4); God's 'healthcare programme' for humanity is Christ who is doctor and medicine and health itself.

> You who are sick take heart, look to your doctor, can you still be without hope? The afflictions were great, the wounds incurable, the illness fatal. You pay attention to the magnitude of the disease, aren't you going to pay attention to the omnipotence of the doctor? You are desperate, but he is omnipotent. The apostles are his witnesses, the first ones healed now proclaim this doctor. Yet even they were healed more in hope than in realization. (*ep. Io. tr.* 8.13)

The incarnation is God's medicine for humanity – and with such a drastic divine intervention, Augustine persistently insists, what must we conclude about the condition of the patient? Within this medical imagery we thus find an important key to understanding Augustine's teaching about and emphasis on original sin. It is not a product of 'Augustinian pessimism', as some are wont to assert, but rather his rhetorically dramatic but nonetheless theologically accurate affirmation of God's diagnosis of humanity revealed in God's 'medicine', the incarnation and redemption by Jesus Christ. Augustine's faith is clear: Christ is humanity's only saving medicine.

The Poor Christ (*Christus Pauper*)

The poor Christ, a third important title, cautions us against turning Augustine's insistence upon Christ as healer into a privatised spirituality. He knew that the Gospel allows for neither purely private nor merely interior journeys. He tells us that no other passage in the gospels moved him as much as Matthew 25:31–46: 'I was hungry and you gave me to eat . . .'

> Brothers and sisters, from time to time I have spoken to you about the Scripture passage that has made the deepest impression on me (*plurimum movet*) and I will continue to remind you often of it. [He goes on to explore Matthew 25 and then comments] I see that you too are moved by this text and that you are surprised (*video etiam vos moveri et mirari*). And it is indeed something that should make us wonder (*vere mira res*). (*s.* 389.5)

The wonder is that the Christ of one's heart is also the Christ of every human relationship, and no human relationship was more privileged than the one that called forth our responsibility towards the poor. Christ's becoming poor and humble demanded that Christians take seriously the broken and hungry Christ in the midst of every human community; it is the poor Christ who is constantly knocking at our door. Augustine's insistence came from his reading of Matthew 25 in the light of Acts 9:4ff.: ' "Saul, Saul, why are you persecuting me?" . . . "I am Jesus whom you are persecuting!" ' For Augustine, Christ's words to Paul asserted his solidarity and identification with the poor, and suffering, in fact, gives them a privileged status. The poor are the empty hands and gaping mouth of Christ in need of our real love – so that incarnation can be said to be bi-directional for Augustine: Christ's becoming flesh is met by our incarnate love for him in the poor!

> Christ who is rich in heaven *chose* to be hungry in the poor. Yet in your humanity you hesitate to give to your fellow human being. Don't you realize that what you give, you give to Christ, from whom you received whatever you have to give in the first place? (*en. Ps.* 75.9)

> Give to your needy brother or sister. To which one? To Christ. Because anyone who is your brother or sister is Christ. And because you give to Christ, you give to God . . . God wanted to be in need before you, and you withdraw your hand? (*en. Ps.* 147.13)

One could say that Augustinian spirituality is always a spirituality of 'solidarity' with the poor Christ holding the privileged place for the solidarity of our love: the poor Christ has come to us; dare we shut our door?

The Whole Christ (*Christus Totus*)

Among the many other titles used by Augustine that of 'the whole Christ' (*Christus totus*) is uniquely developed by Augustine to give his spiritual vision its ultimate horizon. *Christus totus* seeks to express the utter comprehensiveness of Christ, extending from the union of Christ with his church – the Body of Christ – to a profound sense of inclusivity and responsibility that never allows one to separate love of God from love of neighbour, to a culmination in a Christ-centred articulation of humanity's destiny: the one Christ loving himself.

> . . . it is by loving that one becomes a member of Christ, becomes through love incorporated into the body of Christ; and there will be the one Christ loving himself . . . when therefore you love a member of Christ, you're loving Christ, you're loving the Son of God; when you love Christ, you're loving the Son of God, when you love the Son of God you love the Father. Love can never be separated (*non potest ergo separari dilectio*). Choose for yourself what you love and the rest will follow. (*ep. Io. tr.* 10.3)

This insight into the oneness and wholeness of Christ is matched by a call to a oneness and wholeness in our love. It was nourished by his intense engagement with the psalms, which he understood to be the voice of Christ speaking. If the psalms are the voice of Christ, they speak not only Christ's solidarity with us and our solidarity with him but also our solidarity with one another.

> The whole church is made up of all the faithful, because all the faithful are the members of Christ. Thus our Head [Christ] dwells in heaven from whence he governs his body, and while we are separated in terms of vision, we are united in terms of love. Thus the whole Christ is head and body and so in every psalm we hear the voice of the head and the voice of the body. He did not want to speak in a separated way because he did not want to be separated (*noluit enim loqui separatum, quia noluit esse separatus*). He says: 'Behold I am with you always until the consummation of the world.' If he is with us, he speaks in us, he speaks concerning us, he speaks through us; and accordingly we speak in him and indeed we speak the truth because we speak in him. But when we want to speak in our own name and out of our own voice [and not Christ's], we remain in untruth. (*en. Ps.* 56.1)

Shared oneness of life (*in una vita, en. Ps.* 74.4) is what Augustine understands by 'the whole Christ': a hope for as well as statement of true community as grace and promise, present commitment, and ultimately fullness in eternity. It will never cease to challenge Augustine with its boundary-breaking and universalising implications.

If Christ is the way and the homeland (*via et patria*), the Christ we meet on this journey is ever the Christ who is Word, healer, poor and the whole Christ. We find here the focal point and drive of Augustine's spirituality. Indeed Augustine had no doubt that Christ had invited him to undertake a demanding yet fulfilling journey, ever challenged to deeper conversion, ever nourished by delightful moments of intimacy. Untiringly Augustine called upon everyone he encountered to hear their own invitation, knowing that they too would find such delights. He comments on John 1:38–39, where the first disciples encountered Jesus. 'What are you looking for?' Jesus asks. They respond: 'Where are you staying?' Jesus: 'Come and see.' They heard the invitation.

> He showed them where he was staying; they came and were with him. What a happy day they spent, what a happy night! Who is there who can say to us what they learned from the Lord? Let us also build and prepare in our heart a house where he may enter in and teach us and converse with us. (*Io. eu. tr.* 7.9.3)

'Let us also build and prepare in our heart a house where he may enter in and teach us and converse with us.' This remains Augustine's admonition to every human heart. Christ is the foundation of Augustinian spirituality, the heart of the Augustinian tradition; all else flows from here. It will find complement and expression in his insistence on grace, his love of the Bible, his emphasis on interiority, the centrality of love and humility, and its culmination in community – but the journey to the Father always begins with Christ and his promise: 'I am the way.'

A JOURNEY OF GRACE

Christian tradition has bestowed upon St Augustine the title Doctor of Grace, and not without reason. From his day and down to the present his teaching remains the centre point for discussion concerning an authentic theology of grace and its implications for spirituality. In facing this dimension of Augustine's teaching one must keep in mind that his insistence upon the primacy of grace is not first and primarily a speculative or theoretical question. Rather it is an attempt to articulate the Christian experience of humanity before God, learned certainly in his understanding of himself before God. From God's initial free act of creation, to the Son of God's free, loving, and unthinkable becoming incarnate for humanity's redemption, to his very own graced conversion, Augustine exclaimed with Paul: 'What do we have that we have not received?' (1 Corinthians 4:7). And yet dismay is all some have been able to muster before his unyielding insistence that 'all is grace'. While the last two decades of his life were engulfed in debates on the nature and role of grace, called by scholars the Pelagian controversy, his discovery of the centrality of grace occurred early on. Late in life he sums up his position on grace while commenting on a work written shortly after his episcopal ordination: 'In trying to come to a solution I was in favor of the freedom of choice of the human will – but grace won!' (*retr.* II.1). The foundational issue is what matters here for Augustine; he reduces it starkly to this antithesis: are we saved by God's grace or by ourselves (i.e., by our own strength of will)?

To appreciate the power of Augustine's assertion, it is important to note that his mention of 'grace' always implies 'the grace of God through Jesus Christ our Lord' or simply 'the grace of Christ'.[17] For Augustine the issue of grace is simply a consequence of the centrality of Christ for humanity. The emphasis on grace is accordingly a constant reminder that one can never compromise or modify the absolute necessity of salvation and redemption in Christ. Further conditioning and indeed complicating his insistence on grace is the fact that, in the history of Christian theology, Augustine was the first Christian thinker to seriously and deliberately attempt to confront in depth and detail the intersection of divine and human agency, grace and freedom. Metaphysically, but principally theologically speaking, humans as creatures of God can never operate outside of the agency of God the creator. God's radical historical and redemptive intervention in history as the incarnate Word, the incarnate Son of God, only intensifies this affirmation. Augustine is aware that both human experience and reflection affirm that we are equally 'actors' and 'acted upon'. We know that we desire, we deliberate, we choose – positively and negatively. Our 'doing' comes from deep within. But we also know that, in an inexplicable way, not only do we act in the first place, but also from deep within we are moved, attracted, drawn, transformed, repulsed, overwhelmed and even left paralysed. Thus even our freedom remains unfathomable. Above all Augustine's affirmation of grace is simply a manifestation of his persistent rejection of any notion of self-redemption in the exercise of our freedom – and this was certainly Augustine's personal experience.

Whatever we are or do that has salvific implications is, Augustine insists, God's gift. But because it is the grace of God, and the transcendent eternal God is not circumscribed by time or history, God's grace operates upon us in ways that never compromise our integrity. For Augustine, this ever remains mystery: God is eternally just and merciful, omnipotent and transcendent, yet our only true Lover. Augustine does not, cannot, claim to fathom these assertions. In fact, they remain inscrutable: 'Unless you believe, you will not understand' (Isaiah 7:9, LXX). But 'believe' for Augustine was never simply a blind 'yes' to propositions. The heart is the organ of faith and so 'to believe' for Augustine means to discover and respond to the presence of God deep within the human heart. This presence, however, is divine presence, and so never violates us or breaches our integrity and authenticity. God *is* our integrity and authenticity. Even when we choose and decide and commit, God is acting upon us and with us in ways that are humanly inaccessible and impenetrable but, in faith, 'closer to me than I am to myself' (*conf.* 3.7.12). The spirituality of Augustine, with its insistence upon grace, means that we are ever humble and grateful, but certainly not passive or lazy. Once again it is in his preaching and correspondence that this becomes absolutely clear. Here his assertion of the power and mystery of God's grace is complemented by ongoing exhortation to participate in this mystery of grace. He writes to the distinguished Roman lady Proba:

> Everyone must do what they can. If one person is not capable of as much as another, then he or she can still attain it in the other who does have this capability. The condition is that one love and esteem in the other the attainments which one does not have because of one's own limitations. Thus the person with fewer capabilities ought not to impede the person with more; nor should those who are more gifted put pressure on others who are less gifted. You have to render an account of your conscience to God alone. But the only thing that you owe one another is love for one another (Romans 13:8). (*ep.* 130.16.31)

Augustine combines here both humility and activity, finding in love and gratitude the necessary response to the mystery of grace.

GUIDED BY THE SCRIPTURES

One of the most remarkable features of Augustine's *Confessions* is the role which this strikingly original work gives to the Word of God, the Scriptures. The narrative content is so systematically imbued with quotations, images, allusions and the vocabulary of the Scriptures, that in many ways it can be considered a biblical narrative rather than an Augustine narrative. As such, it stands as a lasting monument to the foundational place and action of the biblical word in Augustine's coming to, understanding and living out of the Christian life. The first words of the *Confessions* (1.1.1.) are from Psalm

47:2: 'You are great, Lord, and highly to be praised.' The final words of the work are a paraphrase of Matthew 7:7, a text that occurs again and again throughout Augustine's writings, and provides the rationale for his persistent quest to understand the mysteries of the Word of God: 'Only you', he concludes this lengthy conversation with God, 'can be asked, only you can be begged, only on your door can we knock. Yes, yes indeed, that is how it is received, how it is found, how the door is opened' (*conf.* 13.36.51). But in between these first and final words of the *Confessions* we find him at one moment throwing down the Bible because of its poor prose (3.5.9), snatching it up again to read St Paul (7.21.27), being converted at the Apostle's words (8.12.29), overcome by an insatiable hunger for the psalms (9.4.8), until in Books 11–13 we find him lingering over and lovingly pondering the Genesis account of creation, savouring each word and relishing the wonders he discovers there. 'May your scriptures be my pure delight, so that I am not deceived in them and do not lead others astray in interpreting them' (10.2.3). Augustine has, in his literary artistry, allowed the Word of God so to take over his own words that the two become virtually identical, emblematic of a heart intimately united in love with God in a loving interior discourse. Thus, even when he speaks of himself in his *Confessions*, it is Scripture that is speaking about Augustine (though we need to keep in mind that it is equally Augustine speaking about Scripture); Augustine demonstrates by his practice the absolute centrality and power of the scriptural word for understanding and living the Christian life.

I have already noted his fascination with the image of John resting upon the breast of Jesus at the last supper and drinking in the Word. Augustine felt that same thirst and drew upon all his artistic and rhetorical abilities to awaken it in others. It is clear that for Augustine the biblical word is always infinitely more than the fragile external word written on the equally fragile page; it is only when God speaks directly to the human heart that the scriptural word has truly fulfilled itself. Throughout his life he repeatedly reminds himself and his congregation that while his words reach the ears, God's Word reaches the heart. Scripture is God's handbook, love letter, testament, medicine, contract, road map, judgement: 'You have stricken my heart with your word and I have loved you' (*conf.* 10.6.8). Augustine's spirituality is a biblical spirituality drawn from the Word's profoundest depths, and prominent in this biblical spirituality will be John's gospel, Paul's letters, and the Book of Psalms.

A PILGRIM HEART

Christian iconography often portrays Augustine holding a heart, a flaming heart; in effect the heart has become the trademark of Augustinian spirituality. It arises undoubtedly from his perhaps best-known affirmation of the restlessness of the human heart that opens the *Confessions*: the journey of Augustine is indeed a heart journey. And there is no question that the symbol of the heart holds central place in his efforts to articulate the self. 'My heart is the place where I am whoever I am – *cor meum, ubi ego sum quicumque sum*,' Augustine tells us in his *Confessions* (10.3.4). But it should be kept in mind that what Augustine means to emphasise here is not so much the term 'heart' but all that it represents and evokes. Heart symbolises for Augustine that the God-inspired journey is a graced and ongoing journey that takes us inward, to the interior self, my true self, my God-self, away from what he calls, in classic Pauline fashion, the exterior self (*homo exterior*) (see 2 Corinthians 4:16), our penchant for living 'externally', outside ourselves, committed to a false self, exiled from our truth, clinging to what is transitory. God has stamped the human heart with the divine image (*imago Dei*, Genesis 1:27), an ineffaceable imprint of identity, covenant, dignity and love. Sin disconnects us from that real self, the *imago Dei*, and so we must undertake to return:

> Return to your heart (*redi ad cor*) and see there what you may be thinking about God. For there [at your heart] is

> the image of God. In the interiority of your humanity Christ dwells, there within you are being renewed according to God's image. Recognize its author in the author's image. (*Io. eu. tr.* 18.10)

In the *Confessions* Augustine can say so remarkably to God: 'You were within, it was I who was outside' (10.27.38)! This is the God who is nearer to Augustine than Augustine is to himself (3.7.12).

This call to return to our heart also evokes God's invitation to turn away from the work of a delusionary autonomous self (for Augustine this is synonymous with sin) to the work of God that finds its beginning within our heart, the divine dwelling place. In his work on biblical interpretation, the *De doctrina Christiana*, Augustine calls attention to the rhetorical-grammatical figure called synecdoche, in which the part refers to the whole. That is how Augustine perceives the heart: it refers to our whole self before God. The restlessness of the heart is thus the relentless undertow of the image of God not allowing us to be satisfied by anything less than God. To develop this notion he employs a rich vocabulary: the restless heart, the heart too full (no room for God), the humble heart, the twisted heart (*cor pravum*), the chaste heart, the carnal heart, the sad heart – but most especially the heart intent upon God. A necessary first step in our return to God is to be in touch with the heart (no matter what its condition). 'Up with your heart' (*Sursum cor*), taken directly from the eucharistic Liturgy, is a constant refrain of his preaching and teaching. Its opposite is '*cor in terra*' – Augustine will note how we can drag our 'heart upon the ground' or even bury it, whenever we allow something or someone other than God to become our heart's centre. In a sermon on the psalms Augustine sees Simon Peter as a prime example of a classic heart patient in need of healing. Augustine takes up the conversation between Simon Peter and Jesus at the Last Supper:

> 'I will be with you even if it means death.'
>
> The Lord, however, who [really] knew him, predicted

> that he would fail, foretelling to Peter his own infirmity as if he had reached in and touched the very veins of his heart (*tamquam tacta vena cordis eius*). (*en. Ps.* 36.I.1)

Augustine insists that we too must let God reach in, touch our heart, and make it known to us.

Yet for all of this talk of 'heart', this emphasis on interiority, its intention is never meant to lead to an introverted spirituality. What is fundamentally interior to me is, for Augustine, the point where I am also closest to my brothers and sisters in the human family. From the heart I come to Christian faith, become a member of the church, the Body of Christ, and begin to recognise Christ in my brothers and sisters, with a particular openness of heart for the poor. Heart is that touchpoint where true integration of the interior and the exterior, the spiritual and the incarnational, takes place. Heart is never the final goal, yet what does not start 'from the heart' goes nowhere. Equally true is Augustine's insistence that if something is claimed to be 'in the heart' but never manifests itself outwardly in love and community, it is nothing less than self-deception. His insistence upon the heart is thus not a self-serving escape from responsibility into interior religion and privatised faith. The return to the heart is but the first step of a conversion process that proves itself in universal and unrestricted – catholic – love. Since God has placed God's own image there, it is where we must begin, but it is never the place to end. To come to the heart is simply to discover that we are God's work, that God does dwell within us, that at our deepest and truest level of self we are never alone – and certainly never unloved.

LOVE AND HUMILITY, HUMILITY AND LOVE

As Augustine recounts his spiritual journey in the *Confessions*, he reveals to us his experience of deep inner contradiction. After arriving in Milan, now bearing the title of 'rhetor' in the imperial city, he appears to the casual observer to be accomplished and self-confident. He has been trained never to lose an argument. He is surrounded by devoted students and admirers, declaiming imperial speeches as part of the Milanese court life, well along the path to secure public fame and even more secure private fortune. Yet he insists that the outward image had little in common with his inward distress, a gnawing hunger that increasingly would not allow him to lie to himself that all was well. In fact, lying was precisely the issue. He recounts in Book 6 his preparation for a flattering imperial oration: it was all lies, everyone knew they were applauding lies, and yet everyone would pretend otherwise (6.6.9).

The whole lesson of the *Confessions* was a truth called humility, a self-truth that was not degrading but liberating, since it was always grounded in God's love. In Book 3 he recounts how he took up God's Scriptures looking for wisdom but was not humble enough to learn from them:

> The Bible seemed to be unworthy when I compared it with the dignity of Cicero's writings. My tumor [of pride] turned away from its [humble] approach and my mind was not able to penetrate its depths. Its truth was such that it would grow for those who deigned to be little children but I refused to be such. Swollen [with pride] I seemed to myself to be a very big man. (*conf.* 3.5.9)

Humility, a bitter pill at first resisted, became life-giving medicine, curing the swollenness of his pride. He learned its value from the humble Redeemer (*conf.* 7.18.24), but it was no easy lesson. Strikingly, part of that learning meant he had to even humbly accept his personal stumbling and blindness – never an obstacle for God.

> 'For those who love God, God works all things for good' (Romans 8:28). And this *all* [italics mine] takes in so much that, even if a person deviates from and leaves the right path, he is enabled to make progress in good, for he

> returns more humbled and more experienced. (*corrept.* 9.24)

Augustine came to God more humbled and more experienced, a lesson he never let himself forget nor anyone else. Thus Augustine can sum up the entire Christian life in humility. Writing to Dioscorus in 410/411 he states this with his customary exuberance:

> My Dioscorus, I wish that, with complete piety, you would submit to him and not seek any other way to attaining lasting truth but the one shown us by him who, being God, sees our weakness. This way consists, first, of humility, second of humility, and third, of humility. No matter how often you would ask me, I would say the same. It is not that there are no other precepts to be mentioned. But, unless humility precedes, accompanies, and follows whatever good we do, unless it be a goal ever before us, alongside us to cling to, before us as a restraint, we will find that we have done little good to rejoice in; pride's hand having bereft us of everything. (*ep.* 118.22)

Humility is central to Augustinian spirituality, and once again it is clear that this stance is totally Christ-centred. The humility of the incarnation is the starting point for the humility of the Christian.

Yet Augustine takes the notion of humility to an even more profound plane by vitally linking it to love. 'Where there is humility, there love is' (*ep. Io. tr.*, Prol.). It is the lesson he learned from the incarnation. He gives it a striking application in his treatise on virginity where he cautions lest continence give rise to pride: 'I am concerned lest you act like the Pharisee who arrogantly boasted of his merits . . . I am afraid lest you love little because you think you have little that needs forgiveness' (*virg.* 37.38). Humility is seen by Augustine as the 'door of our heart' which, once opened, allows the Lord to enter in (see *s.* 62A.2). *Superbia* – best translated today as 'arrogance' – is the destroyer of relationship and community, exemplified by the breakdown of the community of Eden: 'The first sin of humanity was arrogance – *primum peccatum hominis superbia fuit*' (see *s*. 159B.5, Dolbeau 21.5). Humility preserves love, it is where love finds its power (see *virg*. 51.52). When we are 'swollen' with ourselves, there is no room left to love God (see *trin*. 8.8.12).

> . . . therefore love with your whole heart him who is beautiful beyond all the sons of men. Gaze upon the beauty of him who loves you . . . Consider how beautiful in him is the very thing for which the proud mock him. With the eyes of your heart gaze upon the wounds of the crucified Jesus, the marks left in the risen Lord, the blood of the dying Christ, the treasure of believers, the price of our redemption! Reflect on how priceless all that is! Place it on the scales of love and weigh it . . . He wants to be wholly fixed in your hearts, he who for your sake let himself be fixed to the cross. (*virg*. 54.55ff.)

Love transforms humility, making it redemptive; humility transforms love, making it universal. It is once again clear that, for Augustine, it is the loving humility and the humble loving of Christ that serves as the measure of all human love and humility. Knowing this love of God generates humility, and knowing true humility enables us to love God, self and others. The opposite of love, for Augustine, is not so much hatred as it is arrogance. It closes us off from God, from others, and even from ourselves.

THE JOURNEYING COMMUNITY

In the garden in Milan, at the precise moment of Augustine's deepest spiritual crisis, we also find close at hand his dearest friend Alypius. Not only was he witness to the event of conversion, but he was its first beneficiary (see *conf*. 8.12.30). Throughout the *Confessions*, as Augustine is offering us a deeply personal story of a spiritual journey, it should be noticed that he is never journeying alone. Friends, cherished friends, are always at hand, and as we learn Augustine's story we also learn theirs. There is a poignant witness to this in the story of the death of a friend in Book Four. He had led the unnamed companion into Manichaeism but, having taken ill and fallen into unconsciousness, he was baptised a Catholic Christian. When the friend regained consciousness Augustine derided the baptism, expecting the same from a compliant friend, but instead received a harsh rebuke: 'If you wish to be my friend, stop saying such things.' Augustine left shattered, but expecting another chance to reclaim his friend – it was not to be.

> . . . he died and I was not there. Black grief closed over my heart and wherever I looked I saw only death. My native land was a torment to me and my father's house unbelievable misery. Everything I had shared with my friend turned into hideous anguish without him. My eyes sought him everywhere, but he was missing . . . (*conf.* 4.8.9)

As Augustine continues to tell of his grief he also introduces us to true friendship: 'He alone loses no one dear to him, to whom all are dear in the One who is never lost' (4.9.14).

There is a tension in Augustine's spirituality that is all too easily misunderstood, or all too easily resolved. There is throughout his writings a striking and provocative sense of the subject, the personal self; yet at the very same time there is an equally striking and provocative sense of shared humanity, shared community. In an otherwise penetrating work on *Jesus and Community* the noted theologian Gerhard Lohfink laments what he sees as Augustine's diverting of ancient Christianity from 'community' to 'individualism'.[18] Does Augustinian spirituality lead to a privatised spirituality? While it is clear that Augustine privileges the heart and the journey within, he would be the first to decry any reading of him that would turn the Christian life into a solitary journey. It is always a shared pilgrimage, a community of fellow believers on a journey of faith to God.

> Let *us* go [italics mine], let *us* go! And they respond: Where are *we* going? The answer: To that place, that holy place. They speak thus to each other and like incense one by one they make one flame. And this one flame created from the igniting of each other carries them up together to that holy place, and holy thought sanctifies them. If holy love thus carries them up to a temporal place, what kind of love is it that carries those who live in harmony up to heaven, saying to one another: Are *we* not going to the house of the Lord? Let *us* run therefore, let *us* run, because *we* are going to the house of the Lord. Let *us* run and not grow weary . . . Let *us* run into the house of the Lord . . . Walk on, run. The Apostles saw this and said *to us*: Run, walk on, follow. (*en. Ps.* 121.2)

There is no denying the eloquence of Augustine's 'thoughts in solitude'. Lohfink, in the work just mentioned, cites one of Augustine's more famous and often repeated 'solitary' affirmations, from a classic 'solitary' work: The *Soliloquies*:

> *Augustine*. Lo, I have prayed to God.
> *Reason*. Now what do you want to know?
> *A*. All those things which I prayed for.
> *R*. Sum them up briefly.
> *A*. I desire to know God and the soul?
> *R*. Nothing more?
> *A*. Absolutely nothing. (*sol*. 2.1)

But for Augustine 'solitude' never means 'individualism'.

Surely no one before Augustine had expressed with equal depth and eloquence such intense concern that Christian spirituality be authentic and from the heart. By his day the church had become as widespread as the empire, and 'respectable'. True faith could all too easily be replaced by religious etiquette and group piety. Public Christianity could substitute for real conversion and real commitment. Often too glibly labelled as Constantinian Christianity, Augustine was indeed dismayed by what he saw as a persistent temptation of a now established

Christian community to settle for exterior faith. His emphasis on 'God and the soul', in fact a very early statement written shortly after his conversion as a young Christian thinker, will mature into a much more expansive understanding of the nature of holiness, but it will never lose sight of the need to start at the level of one's heart. What will become increasingly clear in Augustine's thought is the danger of stopping there. In fact, if one does indeed come to 'know God' and 'to know the soul', that knowledge, Augustine is convinced, will blossom into evangelical love. Once again it is necessary to avoid 'systematising' Augustine as if the eloquent statement from the *Soliloquies* could be seen as the foundation stone of an 'Augustinian system'. Augustine is more complex – and thoughtful – than that.

Clearly, Augustine's emphasis on 'a spirituality of the self' fits into a particular historical context that seemed all too prone to eliminate the necessary tension between self and community. He decried a dualistic and Gnostic Manichaeism that postured as true Christianity and dismantled human autonomy. In response Augustine needed to affirm the goodness and responsibility of each individual. In the face of an aggressive Donatism, the Christian church that rivalled Augustine's Catholic Christian community and seemed, in Augustine's eyes, to leave little room for tolerance and human imperfection, Augustine insisted endlessly on community and communion as necessary signs of an authentic faith journey. Dismayed by a Pelagianism that, for Augustine, anchored salvation all too insecurely in one's own power and willing, he insisted upon the sovereignty of God's grace. God, self and community are inextricably bound together in the spirituality of Augustine. Indeed, Augustine's writings are filled with rhetorical explosions that, if taken by themselves, could suggest either God *or* self *or* community. However, to do so, to remove or isolate or separate God *or* self *or* community within the thought of Augustine would only result in a profound distortion of his spiritual vision. Human responsibility, the demands of community, the sovereignty of God – they do seem to be mutually incompatible. Yet for Augustine they are held together in a delicate though demanding unity.

One of the guiding New Testament narratives for Augustine was that found in the Book of Acts where the first Christian community, the apostolic community of Jerusalem, is described. In Augustine's Latin version of Acts 4:32 this first community was described as 'one in soul and one in heart – *anima una et cor unum*'. Augustine boldly and unapologetically emended this biblical description by adding '*in Deum*' – 'one heart and one soul intent upon God (*cor unum et anima una in Deum*'. It becomes a key phrase for Augustine to describe the church and to describe Christian community at its most intense level. Yet it is built from within – from the heart and from the soul. Augustine daringly qualified that scriptural text with '*in Deum*', I would argue, to leave no doubt that he understood the unity of Christian community to be God-sourced and God-directed. Faith in the risen Lord creates community, and it is in ecclesial community and sacramental communion that faith finds its fulfilment. It is difficult among early Christian writers to find a comparable insistence and intransigence, panegyric and practicality regarding the importance and central role that the church as community plays in the spiritual life of the Christian.

CONCLUSION

Augustine (and his culture) resisted verbal brevity and so it is no easy task to try to consolidate neatly and express briefly in a few key words or dense statements the core of his spirituality, his guiding spiritual vision. He held together seemingly conflicting and competing principles and seemed to revel in the tension this created. Yet to be faithful to that spirituality, its entire horizon must be allowed to remain intact, unwieldy as it often may seem. I have tried to suggest the wide extent of that horizon, realising that even here it is necessary to be selective. More could be said of Augustine's spirituality: its liturgical and sacramental context, the importance he gives to prayer (nourished from the Bible), the centrality of mutual forgiveness, an underlying and intensely Pauline theological anthropology; the spiritual models Augustine presents (Paul the convert, Job the hoper, active Martha and contemplative Mary), its relationship to 'the city', its eschatological dimension – the list could continue. Yet the central themes already explored in this chapter ground even these. What should be clear is that Augustine's spirituality begins with a profound awareness of his and humanity's total dependence upon God, and at the same time with the startling discovery that God calls humanity to intimacy in Christ. For Augustine, this divine involvement with humanity always remained mystery – it seemed to be impossible and unthinkable, except that God's revelation calls us, in our own limited way, to think the unthinkable. And that is precisely what Augustine tried to do, and explains why the Augustinian spiritual tradition is inevitably marked by a tradition of seeking to think out the mystery. However, as a tradition, it will inevitably find itself in difficult straits whenever it forgets, as Augustine never did, that even so, the mystery ever remains beyond human grasp. Augustine concludes his arguably most profound theological exploration, *On the Trinity*, with a prayer, one that serves as a vivid reminder that for him not only are spirituality and theology inseparable, but that both are deeply plunged into the mystery of God, and it is that which fires the journey:

> Directing my attention toward this rule of faith [in the Trinity] as best I could,
> as far as you enabled me to,
> I have sought you and desired to see intellectually what I have believed,
> and I have argued much and toiled much.
> O Lord my God, my one hope, listen to me lest out of weariness I should stop wanting to seek you,
> but let me seek your face always, and with ardor.
> Do you yourself give me the strength to seek,

having caused yourself to be found and having given me the hope of finding you more and more.
Before you lies my strength and my weakness; preserve the one, heal the other.
Before you lies my knowledge and my ignorance;
where you have opened to me, receive me as I come in;
where you have shut to me, open to me as I knock.
Let me remember you, let me understand you, let me love you.
Increase these things in me until you refashion me entirely . . . (*trin.* 15.51; WSA I/5, 436)

2. THE GLUE OF LOVE: A 'RULE' FOR COMMUNITY

Late in life (425), Augustine found himself engulfed in yet another crisis. In confronting it he left to posterity not only a priceless excursion into his autobiography but even more importantly a clear statement of his deepest spiritual aspirations. The crisis concerned a scandal in his monastery of clerics and Augustine felt obliged to address it publicly. In so doing he leaves little doubt that one must know Augustine the monk in order to genuinely understand and appreciate his spirituality.

> I, whom by God's grace you see before you as your bishop, came to this city as a young man; many of you know that. I was looking for a place to establish a monastery, and live there with my brothers. I had in fact left behind all worldly hopes, and I did not wish to be what I could have been . . . So much did I dread the episcopate, that since I had already begun to acquire a reputation of some weight among the servants of God, I wouldn't go near a place where I knew there was no bishop . . . I came to this city to see a friend, whom I thought I could gain for God, to join us in the monastery. It seemed safe enough, because the place had a bishop. I was caught, I was made a priest, and by this grade I eventually came to the episcopate. I brought nothing with me; I came to this church only with the clothes I was wearing at the time. And because what I was planning was to be in a monastery with the brothers, Father [Bishop] Valerius of blessed memory, having learned of my purpose and desire, gave me that plot where

> the monastery now is. I began to gather together brothers of good will, my companions in poverty, having nothing just like me, and imitating me. Just as I had sold my slender poor man's property and distributed the proceeds to the poor, those who wished to stay with me did the same, so that we might live on what we had in common. But what would be our really great and profitable common estate was God himself. (*s.* 355.2)

Augustine's first real home in Hippo Regius, he tells us, was a monastery for his 'brothers of good will, companions in poverty', constructed on a plot of church land given him by Bishop Valerius. It was to substitute for the quasi-monastic community he had gathered together on his family estate in Thagaste and was unexpectedly forced to abandon when called to serve the church as a priest. As he continues the sermon we will discover that the crisis he is facing concerns his 'other' monastery in Hippo Regius. Augustine reminds the gathered faithful of some remote history, that once he became bishop he felt impelled to leave the 'garden monastery' first provided for him by Valerius and move to the bishop's house. The hospitality demanded by a bishop's responsibilities, Augustine tells us, would have compromised the more secluded lifestyle of the original monastic community 'with the brothers'. The episcopal household, however, was not to be an obstacle to Augustine's personal commitment to the monastic life. 'And that is why I wanted to have a monastery of clerics in the bishop's residence. This then is how we live: nobody in our company is allowed to have any private property . . .' (*s.* 355.2). The crisis that provoked this public self-confession was the death of a priest in the monastery of clerics who left a will – a legal act that affirmed that the recently deceased had still claimed private property. This was in flagrant violation of the fundamental commitment that united the religious community Augustine gathered together:

> Now many of you know from holy scripture how we wish to live, and how by God's grace, we already do live; to

> remind you of it, though, the actual reading from the book of the Acts of the Apostles shall be chanted to you, so that you may see where the pattern is described which we desire to follow. (*s.* 356.1)

Augustine had the deacon Lazarus read Acts 4:31–35 to the gathered faithful, a capsule description of the shared way of life of the apostolic community in Jerusalem. When the deacon had finished the reading, Augustine received the Scriptures from him but then did the unexpected:

> I too want to read it. It gives me more pleasure, you see, to be reading these words than to be arguing my case with my own words *(He repeats the text just read from Acts)* . . . You have heard what our wishes are; pray that we may be able to live up to them. (*s.* 356.1–2)

We hear from Augustine's very lips the apostolic and now monastic ideal that guides his manner of living, the way of life of the first Christian community of Jerusalem, a community formed by resurrection faith, 'one soul and one heart – *anima una et cor unum*' (Acts 4:32) in their faith and mutual love. For the living out of that ideal, the concrete fact of shared goods, no personal property and so no possibility of a last will or testament regarding the disposition of goods no longer one's own, was a *sine qua non*. From the earliest days of his post-conversion life the ideal of that first Christian community became the inspiration and model for an Augustinian way of life, the lived context of Augustine's personal vocation and spirituality – that is what we learn from this late-in-life crisis.

AUGUSTINE'S MONASTIC VISION

Surprisingly, Augustine's monastic vision is a foundational aspect of his spirituality that often goes unnoticed, a legacy too little known and regrettably under-appreciated by many students of Augustine. It is the other side of his spiritual vision, the setting where he tried to put that vision into practice, where he strove to make holiness real, where his theology showed itself not as a theory for public disputation but as a practice for living in love. The scriptural source for this living in love, as already noted, was the example provided by the first Christian community in Jerusalem. This ideal also offered Augustine tangible guidelines for what every Christian community should be, and for him they were to be made most manifest in a monastic community. It is this dimension of Augustine's spirituality that we will now explore.

There have been renewed efforts to achieve a better understanding of the origins of early Christian monasticism. Over the centuries much of monasticism's initial aims and development had been lost sight of, impeding accurate understanding of its basic identity and context. Accordingly, much recent scholarship has sought to achieve a more informed appreciation of this critically important dimension of Christian spirituality. Through such research it has become increasingly clear that Augustine's monastic vision has profoundly shaped and influenced all of Western monasticism, notably the fundamental documents of Benedictine monasticism.[1] In turn, we know that Augustine himself was influenced by traditions of Eastern monasticism, channelled not only through his contact with the *Life of Antony* (see *conf.* 8.6.15) but also through other sources, as manifest in his comments about Egyptian monastic prayer traditions in his *Letter to Proba* (*Letter* 130.10.20). It is above all in a little document called *The Rule of St Augustine* that we find expressed Augustine's monastic ideals, a clear statement not only of the theory and practice of monasticism but also of those values and principles we have just explored in Chapter 1 now realised as a lived spirituality.

THE RULE OF St AUGUSTINE

> These are the things we prescribe (*praecipimus*) for your observance in the monastery. Above all else live harmoniously in the house having one soul and one heart intent upon God (*anima una et cor unum in Deum*). Do not call

> anything your own; possess everything in common . . . (*Rule of St Augustine* I.1–3)

With economy of words and loftiness of ideals Augustine thus begins his *Rule*. It is only some three thousand words in length, with emphasis on values rather than details. Despite its brevity it has been the centre of much debate. Before examining the spirituality of Augustine's *Rule* some brief comments are in order regarding some of the reasons for the controversy.

There is a complicated history of disputed questions surrounding the collection of texts associated with Augustine's monastic teaching and thought. The central text in these debates is the document just cited, traditionally referred to as the *Rule of St Augustine*. It has come down in both feminine and masculine versions, and raises a first question regarding whether, in its original form, it was initially intended for men or women. In the course of history the text of the *Rule* was combined with other 'Augustinian' documents (there is as yet little consensus regarding whether all or only some of these texts are truly Augustine's), creating confusion as to the *Rule*'s original form. One of these texts is called the *Obiurgatio*, the word meaning 'reprimand' (found in Augustine's *Letter* 211.5–16); the other is traditionally referred to as the *Ordo monasterii*, as the Latin title implies, an 'order' or set of precepts for living the monastic life. In G. Lawless's *Augustine of Hippo and His Monastic Rule* this 'textual labyrinth'[2] is deftly explored and sorted out, as he draws upon and develops the painstaking manuscript and philological research of the most renowned scholar of the Augustinian *Rule* in the twentieth century, L. Verheijen.

Why have there been controversies about Augustine's *Rule* in the first place? Beyond the question of the feminine and masculine versions as well as the 'textual labyrinth', there is the simple fact that Augustine never tells us 'I wrote a Rule.'

> . . . identification of Augustine as author of a monastic rule occurs for the first time in the *Rule* of Eugippius about one hundred years after Augustine's death. In like

> manner, we must wait more than a century and a half after the bishop of Hippo died until an anonymous scribe identified Augustine as the author of the monastic rule which posterity long associated with his name. (Lawless, *Monastic Rule*, 65)

This was not a problem for most 'Augustinians' of the Middle Ages, who resolved such questions by legends, forgeries, dialectics and iconography. In our time, however, these questions have been subjected to greater historical rigour. Based upon careful philological and textual analysis of hundreds of manuscripts as well as an in-depth study of Augustine's thought and vocabulary, Verheijen has argued for the authenticity of the *Rule of St Augustine* as well as the primacy of the masculine version. He theorises that it was at the precise moment of Augustine's move from the garden monastery to the bishop's residence that he composed the *Rule*: it was a way of continuing an authoritative presence and was not originally intended for publication but solely for the guidance of that little monastic community Augustine loved so dearly but now had to leave. Verheijen further argues that it was Augustine himself who adapted the masculine version for the women's monastery in Hippo Regius and thus it was that a manuscript tradition began to develop according to the two versions. This written tradition was accompanied by oral traditions attributing the *Rule* to Augustine. At least until further evidence emerges or until Verheijen's historical-philological arguments are dismantled, his theory remains the most viable.[3] What has also been strikingly demonstrated by a number of modern critical scholars is the compatibility between everything said in the *Rule of St Augustine* and Augustine's own thought and vocabulary. In an attempt to give a fresh scholarly perspective to the entire question, Verheijen also proposed new terminology for the documents contained in this Augustinian monastic dossier. In particular he proposed that the *Rule* be called the *Praeceptum*, from its opening Latin words that include '*praecipimus*', 'we prescribe or lay down'. I will follow as much as possible Verheijen's terminology in this chapter. With these prolegomena behind us, we can now proceed to lay out what is distinctive about Augustine's monastic vision, noting how it embodies the essential values of his spirituality.

MONASTIC VALUES - GOSPEL VALUES

The *Praeceptum* is a brief but dense document. A present-day division into eight chapters reflects the basic simplicity of its precepts, though underlying that simplicity challenges abound.[4]

1: Purpose and Basis of Common Life
2: Prayer
3: Moderation and Self-Denial
4: Safeguarding Chastity and Fraternal Correction
5: The Care of Community Goods and Treatment of the Sick
6: Asking Pardon and Forgiving Offences
7: Governance and Obedience
8: Observance of the Rule

In a seminal article entitled 'The Evangelical Inspiration of the Rule of St Augustine',[5] van Bavel proposed that Augustine based his monastic vision embodied in the *Praeceptum* upon foundational gospel values: 1) unity of heart; 2) community life as an expression of love, the first commandment of Christ; 3) absolute respect for the person of the other, which follows from a consistent love for one another; 4) humility as the indispensable condition for loving another (only humility can make a person open to others and counteract egoism); 5) community of goods as the realisation of this openness to others (private property offers a constant temptation to live only for oneself) (see van Bavel, 88). Van Bavel suggests that what Augustine offers in his *Praeceptum* is simply a way of gospel living, a way of embodying gospel values and themes such as love, grace, freedom, heart and humility. Where Augustine himself found these values embodied and lived was, as we have already noted, in the first Christian community in Jerusalem, a community formed by faith in the risen Lord, bound together by the deepest bonds of love, whose very existence provided testimony to their faith in the risen Christ. Here was the inspiration, prototype, summons and measure for what each and every Christian community is called to be, an ideal expressed in the most general and the most concrete terms: one mind and one heart, full and complete community of goods.

This archetypal Christian community of post-resurrection Jerusalem was not only at the forefront of Augustine's vision of the monastic life but, even more basically, offered model and ideal for the entire church as a community of faith and love. Thus there is a vital intersection between Augustine's monasticism and the church as a whole. For him this 'Jerusalem community' is embodied both universally in the whole church and locally in its many ecclesial manifestations, from family to monastic community, a dynamic ideal that Augustine frequently emphasises in the course of his preaching.[6] At the precise centre of this sense of community was the affirmation of Acts 4:32: the Jerusalem community was 'one soul and one heart intent upon God – *anima una et cor unum in Deum*'.[7] In these few words Augustine sought to express what every Christian community is called to be.

Furthermore, it ought to be highlighted that both lay and clerical monastic communities founded by Augustine in Hippo Regius were urban communities, visibly inserted into the social fabric of the city. While these 'servants of God'[8] were certainly distinctive in their lifestyle and form of life, they were, nonetheless, closely bound not only to the wider Christian community but to the entire urban population. The *Praeceptum* takes for granted that its community prays with the wider community and mingles in street and shop with that same community, even going to the public baths.[9] Thus its 'oneness of soul and heart intent upon God' was not only inward looking but equally outward reaching. In its very existence this monastic community is ecclesial and 'in the world', neither closed off nor narrowly self-protecting. One might conclude that Augustine calls this indeed unique and concrete community to offer a bold and radical witness to what the entire church is meant to be, not only when gathered for worship but likewise in all of its domestic and social manifestations.[10] Commenting upon Augustine's dynamic addition of '*in Deum*' to Acts 4:32's description of the oneness of soul and heart of that apostolic community, van Bavel remarks:

> Unity, then appears as the necessary requisite for our being on the way towards God with one another. Consequently, God appears in our love for one another; by way of the human we go to God. For true living together presupposes love, and love is ultimately God. (van Bavel, 86)

He notes here Augustine's identification of divine love and human love, a seemingly bold statement if it were not for the fact that he based it on 1 John 4:16 ('God is love'). This is perhaps what is most distinctive about Augustine's *Praeceptum*: its emphasis on love as the monastic ideal – not withdrawal, not asceticism, not obedience, not even prayer; it all comes down to love, and as will be seen, this love must be practical and neighbourly.

A COMMUNITY OF LOVE

To understand the radical centrality of love in the *Praeceptum* one need only glance at key points in its brief chapters.

Chapter I

Augustine expresses a concern for the challenges of diversity within the monastery, where the rich and well-educated form one community with the poor and illiterate; this document is dealing with the real problems of a concrete group of people – it is not a theoretical work. Augustine lays out a variety of tensions caused by such a taxing interface. While reproving excesses on both sides, the final solution takes the form of a religious exhortation to love: 'Let everyone live together in oneness of mind and heart, and honor God in yourselves whose temples you have become' (I.8). Augustine asserts the identification of the love of God with the love of the neighbour, comprehending both loves in a veritable liturgical framework with his temple imagery.

Chapter III

Augustine again speaks of diversity, this time of needs within the community based upon differences of health and social status, a source of tensions and jealousies. But he does not propose a 'flattening out' of differences so that everyone is treated the same; rather, he shows great sensitivity to the uniqueness of the individual while maintaining a never-ending call to 'the higher ideal'. Thus Augustine admonishes: 'Nor should all want to receive what they see given in larger measure to the few, not as a token of honor, but as a help to support them in their weakness' (III.4). Love is tailored to the real needs of the individual, even to weaknesses. Yet even those with special needs must not let their love of God grow soft:

> When they have recovered their former strength, they should go back to their happier way of life which, because their needs are fewer, is all the more in keeping with God's servants. Once in good health, they must not become slaves to the enjoyment of food which was necessary to sustain them in their illness. For it is better to need less than to have more. (III.5)

Chapter IV

Augustine highlights mutual responsibility, in particular, faithfulness to chastity. Once again it is presupposed that these servants of God will be in contact with members of the opposite sex. One has to imagine not only the volatile Mediterranean temperament easily awakened to passion but also that of the North Africans, a culture that seemed to thrive on hot-blooded display.[11] What Augustine proposes is a mature and demanding love where mutual responsibility is to be a fraternal wall of support and security around each individual member of the community.

> So when you are together in church and anywhere else where women are present, exercise a mutual care over purity of life. Thus, by mutual vigilance over one another will God, who dwells in you, likewise take care of you by means of each other. (IV.6)

What follows then is a worst-case scenario. If someone appears to be romantically 'involved', it is not love but cruelty that turns a blind eye. The issue is to be brought discreetly to the attention of the appropriate authority but it is clear that those so doing must be motivated by mercy and not by anything else:

> Indeed, yours is the greater blame if you allow your brothers to be lost through your silence when you are able to bring about their correction by your disclosure. If your brother, for example, were suffering a bodily wound that he wanted to hide for fear of undergoing treatment, would it not be cruel of you to remain silent and a mercy on your part to make this known? (IV.6)

Augustine is envisioning here a mature and nuanced form of love that does not allow a brother to be lost under the guise of a mistaken tolerance. It may sound jarring to modern ears, more used to a 'live and let live' principle as a guide to human relationships, to hear Augustine thus conclude:

> And let everything I have said about not fixing one's gaze [on women] be also observed carefully and faithfully with regard to other offenses: to find them out, to ward them off, to make them known, to prove and punish them – all out of love for the man and a hatred for the sin. (IV.10)

One sees here a theme that runs throughout Augustine's writings: love for one's brother or sister can never be blind to the importance of their holiness and salvation. Perhaps here modern readers may find themselves particularly challenged by Augustine's unambiguous clarity regarding what holiness can and cannot allow or tolerate.

Chapter VI

Augustine faces the question of conflict in his monastic community. His approach confronts the practical realities of people from different backgrounds and social realities trying to achieve 'oneness of heart and mind intent upon God'. 'You should either avoid quarrels altogether or else put an end to them as quickly as possible' (VI.1). Remarkably, Augustine does not suppose a quarrel-free community; his knowledge of the human propensity to succumb to weakness and patent selfishness suggests that what is more important is to aspire to the ideal of being a reconciliation-minded community. This is precisely what Augustine lays out as he continues the admonition just cited: '. . . otherwise, anger may grow into hatred, making a plank out of a splinter, and turn the soul into a murderer. For so you read: "Everyone who hates his brother is a murderer" (1 John 3:15)' (VI.1).

As we have seen, Augustine's works are shot through and through with biblical quotes and allusions. The *Praeceptum* is a veritable scriptural tapestry. Verheijen, in his critical edition, provides a list with 216 scriptural quotes and allusions in this short text of 247 lines.[12] As the monastic community read aloud and together heard Augustine's words, what they were really hearing was a rich and biblically inspired call to holiness. As in the passage from the *Praeceptum* just cited, a scriptural text is often used with great force; in this case it is to remind the members of this community of the devastating consequences of unforgiveness.

As he continues he surely has also in mind his own intensive christological explorations of the work of Christ the healer (*Christus medicus*) when he invites the servants of God to share in dispensing Christ's medicinal love: 'Don't exchange harsh words, but if your words do hurt, let your own words become a medicine to heal the wound' (VI.2). Forgiveness in this community is, it may be said, the actualisation of a healing love. Thus the ultimate goal of love that is at the centre of this monastic community is never lost sight of, as specific 'virtues' such as forgiveness are drawn into its dynamic.

Chapter VII

Obedience is likewise placed forcefully into the same framework of love, for the one entrusted with the responsibility of governance as well as for the individual members of the community. All are invited to understand both authority and obedience as the activity of love:

> The one placed over the community should not think himself fortunate because he can dominate by power but rather because he can serve in love . . . he should strive to be loved by you rather than feared, ever mindful that he must give an account of you to God. (VII.3)

> It is by being obedient, therefore, that you show mercy not only towards yourselves, but also towards the superior whose higher rank among you exposes him all the more to greater peril. (VII.4)

There is a mutuality between authority and obedience: authority must be an expression of service rather than power, obedience an expression of mercy rather than compliance. Thus while Augustine's *Praeceptum* can seem quite simple and concise, underlying its succinct precepts is an exacting and challenging call to the boldest claims of evangelical love. Throughout the *Praeceptum* we have seen the same underlying approach: seemingly simple 'precepts' are grounded in and manifestations of demanding gospel living. Virtually each statement is linked to an ongoing call for deepening conversion and presupposes a constant need for God's grace. It is for this reason that students of Augustine's *Praeceptum* are constantly seeking to uncover its dense substratum as a key to understanding its fundamental message and intent.

This is the case with Lawless's proposal that there are nine 'enduring values' embedded within the *Praeceptum*'s precepts and exhortations: God-centredness, inwardness, single-mindedness, grace and freedom, prayer, common life, harmony in the house, fraternal correction, love of spiritual beauty. He also notes that these are 'characteristic of Augustinian thought generally'.[13] Augustine's monasticism is simply a more focused expression of his overall spirituality.

Both Lawless's and van Bavel's interpretative keys also serve as a reminder that the *Praeceptum* invites a variety of approaches. This adaptability or flexibility, in the sense that it emphasises core values rather than precise behaviours, remains an important dimension of Augustine's monastic vision and indicates why it subsequently became such an influential text. Augustine is proposing what he sees as essential gospel values rather than fixed practices. Because of this emphasis on values, those religious communities who follow the Augustinian *Praeceptum* demonstrate remarkable diversity and find it even today a vital statement of deep religious commitment.

MONASTIC WISDOM

Before Augustine ever considered the monastic life he spent years in rhetorical training and eventually practised the art of persuasion with great success. He knew the power, both helpful and dangerous, of words. Though Augustine abandoned the chair of rhetoric in Milan, he did not totally abandon his rhetorical past. One of the striking dimensions of his ability to express the demands of Christian living was the art with which he could express them in eloquent, memorable and often provocative ways. The *Praeceptum* is filled with such gems of wisdom, loaded maxims that both teach and challenge. And this gift for memorable aphorism runs deep throughout all of

Augustine's writings, suggesting that behind it lies something more than the clever or coincidental cast of a phrase.

Writing to the noble woman Proba on prayer (*Letter* 130), he reveals his knowledge of the desert monks of Egypt, including their unique approach to prayer.

> It is said that the brothers in Egypt have certain prayers which they recite often, but they are very brief, and are, so to speak, darted forth rapidly like arrows, so that the alert attention, which is necessary in prayer, does not fade and grow heavy through long-drawn-out periods. By this practice they show quite well that, just as this attention is not to be awakened if it cannot be sustained, so, if it can be sustained, it is not to be broken off too quickly. (*ep.* 130.10.20)

Augustine here calls attention to the Egyptian monastic practice of using brief formulas in order to maintain attention and commitment to prayer. It was, without doubt, a practice he also knew well from his years as an orator who had to maintain the attention and commitment of his audience. It continued to manifest itself throughout his writing and preaching where he sums up complicated questions and explorations with brief and almost poetic declarations:

> Shared was our loss, shared be our finding – *communis fuit perditio, sit communis inventio.* (*s.* 115.4.4)

> Love and do what you will. (*ep. Io. tr.* 7.8)

> Listen to me, you who are poor: is there anything you do not possess when you possess God? And listen to me, you who are rich: do you possess anything when you do not possess God? (*s.* 311.15)

> Possess love, and you possess everything. (*Io. eu. tr.* 32.8)

> Where humility reigns, there is love. (*ep. Io. tr.* Prol.)

> When does prayer fall silent? When desire grows cold. (*s.* 80.7)

> It is better to love and be hard than to be gentle and cause harm. (*ep*. 93.4)

> When you consider yourself to be the final end of all, then that is the final end of you. (*ep. Io. tr.* 10.5)

> Our daily cleansing, the Lord's prayer – *Quotidiana nostra mundatio, Dominica oratio*. (*s*. 261.10)

In the first and last examples, one gets the poetic flavour of Augustine's Latin prose. These little sayings, all of which occur in the course of Augustine's preaching, were designed to summarise ideas, hold audience's attention, and in their very poetic brevity embed themselves effortlessly upon heart and mind. They were easily remembered and so could be readily called to mind to provoke continuing reflection, prayer and vigilance. This practice meshes easily with the pregnant wisdom sayings of the desert fathers and mothers, the *Apophthegmata* – and, in turn, these practices of ancient Christianity draw upon a rich wisdom tradition reflected both in Old Testament wisdom literature and classical authors such as the Stoic thinker Seneca with his sometimes witty but always serious aphorisms.

The *Praeceptum* is rich in lapidary statements that sum up Augustine's monastic ideal and provide a basis for ongoing reflection and prayer. They offer a perspective regarding how these ideals were meant to be kept alive, suggesting a spiritual practice of reflective, prayerful rumination throughout the day. A few more examples will suffice. The first is perhaps most noteworthy, since it suggests how the rest were to be employed, by turning them over again and again within one's heart:

Prayerful hearts:

> When you pray to God in psalms and hymns, turn over in your heart what you bring forth with your voice. (II.3)

Regarding arrogance in doing good:

> Every other kind of evil is to be found in the commission of evil deeds, pride (*superbia*) however infects even good deeds in order to destroy them. (I.7)

Fraternal love as a form of worship:

> Let everyone live together in oneness of mind and heart, and honor God in yourselves whose temples you have become. (I.8)

Table manners (reading is done at meals):

> Let not your mouths alone take food, but let also your ears be hungry. (III.2)

Simplicity of life:

> It is better to need less than to have more. (III.5)

A 'fashion statement':

> Don't let your garb be noticeable, seek not by clothing but by life-style to please. (IV.1)

Chaste living:

> Do not claim your mind is pure when your eyes are impure: impure eyes are a sign of an impure heart. (IV.4)

Mutual responsibility:

> Exercise a mutual care over purity of life. Thus, by mutual vigilance over one another will God, who dwells in you, likewise take care of you by means of each other. (IV.6)

The common good:

> You can measure your progress by your growth in concern for the common good rather than your private good. (V.2)

Healing words:

> Don't exchange harsh words, but if your words do hurt, let your own words become a medicine to heal the wound. (VI.2)

Authority and love:

> The one placed over the community should not think himself fortunate because he can dominate by power but rather because he can serve in love. (VII.3)

The call and demands of the *Praeceptum*, it is easy to see, are lofty and require radical self-emptying. It was written for a broad spectrum of monks, some of whom came to Augustine's monastery poor and illiterate, others rich and cultured. These sporadic and poetic aphorisms could keep its monastic ideals fresh in their hearts and minds and serve as a constant reminder that what was being proposed was not so much a set of laws to be observed but, rather, gospel values to be incarnated. This was never to be taken for granted. Augustine is well aware of this as he brings the work to its conclusion:

> May the Lord grant that you observe all of these things with love, as lovers of spiritual beauty, with the fragrance of Christ radiating from your good living, not as slaves under the law but as freedmen established under grace. (VIII.1)

Augustine encapsulates here his insistence that all is grace, a theology of grace intrinsically tied to love, with its source and end in Christ. The final words of the *Praeceptum* remind these servants of God that they are a Christ-community with a mission to bear witness to Christ for the church and world.

If Verheijen is correct that Augustine wrote the *Praeceptum* to provide for his continued spiritual authority over this community no longer enjoying his physical presence, it is clear that they would hear in each word and phrase resonances of previous conversations, sermons, dialogues and admonitions:

love, spiritual beauty, the fragrance of Christ, law and slavery, grace and freedom – these are ideals that form the fabric of Augustine's spiritual vision and will continue to be explored and deepened throughout his life. As Augustine proposes a weekly listening to the *Praeceptum* so that it can serve 'as a kind of mirror' for looking into their life together, his final words ring true to his abiding spiritual vision:

> Where you find that you have been doing what is written here, give thanks to God the bestower of all good gifts. Where, however, one of you finds himself lacking in some things, be sorrowful for what is past and careful about what is to come, praying for forgiveness, and not be led into temptation. (VIII.2)

The final words are not Augustine's but those of the Lord's Prayer (Matthew 6:12–13), a prayer that he constantly recommended to every single Christian as a necessary companion until the end of life (see for example, *civ.* 21.22). These concluding words remind us that Augustine's monastic vision is, indeed, a focused statement of what holds true for the life of every Christian.

The *Praeceptum* is complemented by a host of other writings by Augustine which supplement its concise statement of monastic spirituality. In his *Letter* 48 he insists on monasticism's ecclesial responsibility; in his commentary on Psalm 132 he argues for its evangelical authenticity; in his commentary on Psalm 99 he insists that the monastery is no haven for the perfect; but most especially in his already-cited *Sermon* 355 (and its companion *s.* 356) he passionately proclaims how close to his heart's desire is the monastic life – and how much it is intended to benefit not just the monk but the church: 'We live here with you, and we live here for you; and my intention and wish is that we may live with you in Christ's presence forever' (*s.* 355.1).

CONCLUSION

Perhaps what remains most arresting about Augustine's monastic spirituality is its evangelical simplicity, combined with his deft inserting of individual striving for holiness into a strongly communal context, and a persistent emphasis on grace and love. Here is to be found its attractiveness, another reason why it has been taken up by so many different religious communities over the centuries. If Chapter 1 of this study offered Augustine's spiritual vision, this chapter shows what that vision became in practice. Its powerful model was the Jerusalem community and that community's 'oneness of heart and soul intent upon God' that manifested itself in humility regarding oneself and unselfish love regarding the other. And Augustine never forgot that this practice was both a consequence of and testimony to resurrection faith.

Since the *Praeceptum*'s ideal pertains to the whole church, Augustine's vision of the monastic community witnesses to what all Christian communities are called to be: God-centred, love-driven, dwelling places of forgiveness and healing, nourished by the Word, 'honoring God in one another whose temples we have become'. Augustine often talked of love as a kind of glue (see, e.g., *trin.* 10.2; *s.* 349.2), and it is committed love that holds this community together, despite differences, hurts, human failings and even sin. Augustine's monastic living became the concrete embodiment of his spirituality. It serves as a constant reminder that to do justice to a tradition that bears his name one must be true to the whole Augustine, including Augustine the monk, and it is precisely his monastic tradition that will be considered in the next two chapters.

3. TO TEACH BY WORD AND EXAMPLE: CANONICAL SPIRITUALITY AND THE APOSTOLIC LIFE

As Augustine lay dying, his beloved Catholic Christian and monastic communities of Hippo Regius were under siege: an enemy fleet of the Vandals was blockading his port city. Subsequent to his death these Vandals overran Roman Africa and inaugurated a slow process of turmoil and transition: Byzantine re-conquering, invasions of the seventh and following centuries, leading to the virtual extermination of Christianity in what had been Augustine's Africa. Yet the death of Augustine and these subsequent events did not mean an end to Augustine's impact. Even during his lifetime many of his works had already begun to be widely diffused and read and at his death his library was bequeathed to the church of Hippo Regius.[1] Somehow the library survived the Vandal invasion and eventually found a safe haven on European soil, ensuring that his vast output, contained now in volumes of manuscripts, would continue to speak.

This chapter will pass over nearly seven hundred years of history to concentrate on an Augustinian revival of the twelfth century, exemplified by the Victorine congregation outside Paris, established by William of Champeaux in 1108. 'Exemplified' is a deliberately chosen term since the Victorines are one of a number of 'Augustinian episodes' during a period of transformation and renewal that saw the likes of Bernard of Clairvaux and the Cistercians, and the reform movement of the Canons (the community of St Ruf at Avignon, Ivo of Chartres, Norbert of Xanten and others). Augustine was by no means forgotten during the centuries that separate Augustine and the Victorines. Fulgentius of Ruspe, Eugippius, Prosper of Aquitaine, Isidore of Seville, Caesarius of Arles, Boethius, Gregory the Great, John the Scot, Gottshalk – each was a dedicated student of Augustine, each to greater or lesser degree left his imprint upon a developing Augustinian tradition. Augustine, all commentators agree, was virtually omnipresent throughout the centuries of transition as Western Christianity moved from Late Antiquity into the world of the developing Middle Ages. Bernard McGinn has shown, for example, how Benedictine monasticism took to itself Augustine's theological anthropology and served as the vehicle for its preservation and transmission.[2]

Yet this world was no longer Augustine's world, with its sense of universality created by the Roman Empire and its strong cultural-intellectual ties to the Graeco-Roman world. Augustine's spiritual tradition, with its inherent biblical, theological and philosophical underpinnings, was channelled through fresh biblical, theological and philosophical developments within Western Christianity that provided a new milieu within which Augustine was read, studied and handed on. These new contexts were often quite dissimilar from those Augustine would recognise – and to them we now turn.

IN SEARCH OF THE APOSTOLIC LIFE

The eleventh and twelfth centuries were times of ferment in the West. There were movements afoot to revitalise the life of the church, closely linked with calls for the reform of the clergy. There were repeated denunciations of a monasticism that had, at least in some notorious instances, strayed far from its original ideals and had become a bastion of wealth and political power. In this time of crisis there was, not surprisingly, a glance backward to times that were viewed as more pristine as well as more authoritative. It is thus that the twelfth century heard an increasingly insistent cry to return to 'the apostolic life – *vita apostolica*', that first age of faith, considered the undisputed reservoir of authenticity and integrity. This call was supported by recourse to the patristic tradition, seen as a faithful transmitter and embodiment of those ancient ways of holiness and faith. Given his already pervasive presence within the tradition, Augustine's writings were seen as an important source for renewal. Here was someone who embodied the 'apostolic life – *vita apostolica*'.

Most notably, various reform movements associated with canons (clergy attached to a particular church) turned explicitly to the Bishop of Hippo. Though the history of the canonical movement is complex and varied, one form it took was that of a group of priests with vows living together. Within their numbers some were taken deeply by the call to return to the apostolic life and found in Augustine's *Rule* and his *Sermons* 355–6, 'on the clerical life' (a portrayal of bishop and clerics united together in living the apostolic life) a charter for a renewed way of life. The model of the first apostolic community presented in these texts was seen as sure guide for an authentic holiness of life. Here reformers found both a solid framework for religious living and substantial flexibility for adoption and adaptation of Augustine's evangelical values to a radically new spiritual context. Throughout Europe, reformed foundations of canonical communities which adopted the Augustinian model sprang up. In the process something else also happened. In their assumption of these Augustinian ideals they gradually began to identify with Augustine himself, eventually seeing themselves as his authentic heirs, and like him living in and ministering out of a 'monastery of clerics – *monasterium clericorum*' (*s.* 355.1). By taking up this specific dimension of Augustine's spirituality the canons eventually came to see themselves as heirs to and preservers of the Augustinian tradition.

Discussion continues regarding the exact nature of canonical spirituality and the impact it exerted upon its age, a question that goes beyond the scope of this study. The primary concern here is how to understand the way in which the canons saw themselves as faithful sons and heirs of Augustine. Typical of this sense are the following comments that come from the Prologue to the *Customs of Prémontré*, a document of the Premonstratentians or Norbertines, founded by St Norbert.

> Since the *Rule* [*of St Augustine*] lays down that we should have only one heart and one soul in the Lord it is proper that living under this same rule, bound by the vows of the same profession, we should find ourselves equally unanimous in observing our canonical rule, so that the unity which we ought to preserve in our hearts should be vivified and represented to others by the uniformity of our customs. But it is perfectly clear that to be able to practice this observance and to keep it always in mind most fittingly and in its totality, what ought to be done should be written down. Thus each one can learn from the testimony of a text the manner in which he ought to live, and no one will be able of his own volition to change, to add, or to diminish that which should be done. For it is necessary that we be wary, lest by neglecting the least detail we should progress toward decadence. (*De antiquis ecclesiae ritibus* III)[3]

Clearly in evidence here are what are generally considered to be the leading characteristics of canonical spirituality: an emphasis on the singular authority of Augustine, especially his *Rule*, complemented by a written customary (a collection of guidelines and instructions) that offers a more detailed and identifiable way of life, unique to the origins and intentions of each particular canonical foundation. Thus the above excerpt emphasises Augustine's 'oneness of mind and heart' now actualised by the particular customs of a Norbertine way of life.

But what we also find here is a firm emphasis upon what has been proposed as the distinctive mark of the canonical movement, what is innovative and unique about it. Their living of the *Rule of St Augustine* is meant to be 'represented to others'. This is what one of the leading scholars of the movement, Caroline Walker Bynum, has sought to demonstrate: that what distinguishes it from the traditional monastic spirituality of the previous centuries is that the canonical way of life is intended 'to teach others by word and example' (*docere verbo et exemplo*).[4] Bynum argues that this explicit outward-looking intention contrasts sharply with a monasticism that did not see itself as having an explicit educative function, either within or outside the monastery (see also Vicaire, 85). Augustine the bishop provided not only the model for this spirituality but the authority of his name.

THE VICTORINES

Perhaps the most widely influential canonical movement was that of the Victorines. In 1108 William of Champeaux, archdeacon of Notre Dame and renowned teacher, abandoned the urban setting of Paris for a life of contemplation just outside the walls of the city in an abandoned chapel dedicated to St Victor, martyr. This foundation marked the beginning of a religious-intellectual movement whose fame would spread throughout Europe, the Canons of St Victor, or simply, the Victorines. William's efforts were directed toward both personal and priestly reform, the content for which he found in Augustine's *Rule*: life in common, the renunciation of personal property, the study of Scripture, holiness of heart, an emphasis on contemplation. To these monastic values the Victorine movement added a firm commitment to intellectual inquiry, providing a fertile setting for pursuing the theological, religious and philosophical questions and ideas of the day. This dual Victorine emphasis, religious living and scholarly inquiry, represents what is particularly unique about their relationship with Augustine, their chosen spiritual father.[5] On the one hand they were totally dedicated to his ancient *Rule*, yet at the same time they were deeply involved in theological and intellectual currents that were particular to their age. Of the two greatest Victorine writers, Hugh of St Victor (d. 1141) and Richard of St Victor (d. 1173), Hugh is the most organically 'Augustinian' in his thought. A few brief excerpts from his work will suggest just how close his thought was to his spiritual master.

His book *On the Moral Ark of Noah* became, even in Hugh's lifetime, a classic guide for living out and making progress in the contemplative life. In this work Hugh draws upon and develops the dynamism of Augustine's restless heart (*conf.* 1.1.1) to portray the contemplative thrust of the human heart:

> Thus, once it had begun to lose its integrity through its earthly desires, the human heart, which had hitherto kept its stability in cleaving to divine love and remained one in the love of the One, was, as it were, divided into as many channels as there were objects that it craved, once it had begun to flow in different directions through earthly longings. And that is how it happens that the soul, not knowing how to live its true good, is never able to maintain its stability. Failing to find what it longs for in those things which it has, its desire is always reaching out in pursuit of the unattainable; and so it never has rest. Therefore, from movement without stability is born toil without rest, travel without arrival; so that our heart is always restless till such time as it begins to cleave to him, in whom it may both rejoice that its desire lacks nothing, and be assured that what it loves will last eternally. (*On the Moral Ark of Noah*, 2)[6]

Hugh's analysis is deeply Augustinian with its emphasis upon heart, desire, longing, love, yearning for the One, journey, restlessness. His exploration of these components is intended to provide a guide for the contemplative journey and its tasks. Yet Hugh goes far beyond Augustine, for he incorporates these themes into an explicit programme and framework more comprehensive than that found in Augustine. Hugh was being true to his twelfth-century world and the formulations and needs of its theology and spirituality which sought a more organised, defined, and clearly labelled pathway of faith and prayer. Though Augustine's world had not yet felt this need, seven hundred years of Christian history, the new demands of the medieval church, did call for such precision. Throughout this work Hugh shows that he has read Augustine – there are explicit references to Augustine's commentary on the Psalms and on John's gospel. He also takes up the Bishop of Hippo's passionate concern for the 'vision of God – *visio Dei*', the human longing to 'see God', the intense desire for divine–human intimacy. Hugh's expanded exploration of the nature of this 'seeing' shows both his deep affinity with the Augustinian tradition as well as the novel context in which he operates, once again necessitating a detailed adaptation and more precise elaboration not required by Augustine's world.

His 'On the Nature of Love' (*De Substantia Dilectionis*) likewise shows a profound Augustinianism.

> A single spring of love, welling up within us, pours itself out in two streams. The one is the love of the world, cupidity; the other the love of God, charity. The human heart is in fact the ground from which, when inclination guides it towards outwards things, there springs that which we call cupidity; although, when its desire moves it towards that which is within, its name is charity. There are, then, two streams that issue from the fount of love, cupidity and charity. And cupidity is the root of every evil, and charity the root of every good. So all that is good derives from it, and from it every evil comes. Whatever it may be, then, it is a great force in us, and everything in us derives from it, for this is why it is love. (*De Substantia Dilectionis*, *Spiritual Writings*, 187)

In this little exhortation on true love, expressed through the prism of 'the two loves', most famously explored in Augustine's *City of God* but echoed throughout his writings (see, e.g., *civ.* 14.28; *en. Ps.* 64.2), Hugh demonstrates once again his debt to the Bishop of Hippo. He likewise takes up Augustine's persistent emphasis on the need to turn from the 'outward' to the 'inward', that is, to the heart: to the extent that we desire and cling to the outward and external, we find ourselves alienated from love. Thus the attainment of authentic love must always begin with an inward journey. In this brief but rich meditation Hugh likewise draws upon another Augustinian theme, the 'ordering of love'.[7] In citing Song of Songs 2:2 ('he has ordered love within me') Augustine found the necessary scriptural basis for his exploration of and insistence upon the conversion or ordering of our love towards God. Hugh takes up this Augustinian theme.

> Set charity in order, then, that desire may run from God, and with God, and unto God, from our neighbour and with our neighbour, but not unto our neighbour; from the world, but neither with it nor unto it. And in God alone let it find rest through joy; for, if it is [true] joy, then love may truly rest; if it is [true] desire, then love is running rightly. For [true] love, as we have said, is an affection of the heart (*dilectio cordis*) towards something for the sake of something, desire in its longing for the thing and joy in the thing's enjoyment, running to it and resting in it. This is charity set in order, and all that we do apart from this is not ordered charity (*ordinata charitas*), but inordinate cupidity (*inordinata cupiditas*). (*Institutiones in decalogum legis dominicae*, IV, *De substantia dilectionis et charitate ordinata*, PL CLXXVI, col. 18)

Hugh meticulously lays out in Augustinian fashion the divine dynamics of love. He is equally meticulous in spelling out its antithesis, namely cupidity (*cupiditas*), understood here as 'disordered love'. As Hugh describes it, love is radically theocentric. It flows out from God and returns to God. It is this divine love that resources neighbourly love, so that, in a remarkable reversal, it does not lead us to forget the neighbour but is, in fact, the only sure guarantee that the love we offer our fellow human is itself an ordered love, selfless and true. Within this deeply Augustinian perspective Hugh offers a sure path for the contemplative journey, a progression away from a carnal heart and to the loving vision of God (*visio Dei*).

Richard of St Victor, on the other hand, emerges as a more original and profound mystical thinker, as recognised by the impact his writings had on the medieval contemplative tradition. In this sense it might be said that his Augustinianism is more subtle than Hugh's. There is less quoting but perhaps deeper comprehension. Following in the Victorine tradition his writings are imbued with Scripture, directed towards a deep interiority, grounded in an ordered love (as was Hugh's), deeply committed to the intellectual underpinnings of contemplation, and intended 'for the building up of the Body of Christ'.[8] This last comment reflects what, as has been noted, is a distinct concern for canonical spirituality: to teach others by word and example. Froelich points out the 'verbal and thematic presence' of Augustine in Richard's contemplative writings: 'Charity and wisdom play a central role, as does the enjoyment of God as the goal of contemplation.'[9] Thus, while Augustine is not always visible in the form of an abundance of quotations or explicit references, he is present in the very fabric and dynamism of Richard's thought: 'A person enters into the first tabernacle when he returns to himself. A person enters into the second tabernacle when he goes beyond himself. When going beyond himself, surely a person is elevated to God.'[10] Without doubt Richard has spent much time pondering Augustine's many admonitions in this regard such as the following comment from one of his homilies:

> By abandoning God and loving yourself you have left yourself, and now you set greater value on what is outside than on yourself. Return to yourself (*redi ad te*), but when you have returned to yourself ascend, do not remain in yourself. First return to yourself, away from what is outside, and then return to him who made you, and while you were lost sought you, and while you were fleeing found you, and while opposing him converted you to him. Return, then, to yourself (*redi ergo ad te*), and go to him who made you. Imitate that younger son (see Luke 15:11–32), because, perhaps, you are [that son]. (Augustine, *s.* 330.3)

The mention of the son reminds us that the theme of the return journey of the Prodigal Son finds prominent place in

Augustine's writings. Richard too will take it up as a perennial call to undertake the interior journey that leads to God:

> For truly, we are led outside ourselves in two ways: At one time we are outside ourselves, but we are raised above ourselves. In the former we are taken captive by mundane things; in the latter we are brought back to supermundane things. But just as there is a twofold going out, so there is also a twofold return. From both goings out we return as it were to the dwelling place of our usual life, when after worldly labors or, preferably, after a manifestation of celestial contemplations, we bring the eyes of our mind back to the consideration of our morals, and through investigating our innermost being we examine by studious reconsideration what sort of persons we are ourselves. That which is read concerning the prodigal son in the Gospel is rightly understood with regard to the first return since when he returned to himself, he said, 'How many of the hired servants in my father's house abound with bread, while I perish with hunger in this place?' (Luke 15:17). (*Richard of St Victor*, 'The Mystical Ark' VIII, 320–1)

Richard's comments are thoroughly Augustinian.

EXPOSITION OF THE RULE OF ST AUGUSTINE

Both Hugh and Victor were devoted students of Augustine, but it is arguably the Victorines' attention to the *Rule of St Augustine* and their dedication to Augustine's monasticism that provides the most explicit link between their spiritual movement and their spiritual father. The *Exposition of the Rule of St Augustine*, for many centuries wrongly attributed to Hugh but indisputably coming from the Victorine tradition,[11] made a profound impact upon subsequent efforts to live the Augustinian *Rule*.

These precepts which follow are called a 'rule' because in

> them a norm for right living is to be found. A 'rule' refers to something which rightly governs or rightly teaches. And what we call a 'rule' the Greeks call a 'canon'. This is why those who are established in monasteries according to the regular precepts of the holy fathers and living canonically and according to an apostolic way of life are called 'regulars', or, after the Greek, 'canons'. (*Exposition of the Rule of St Augustine* I)[12]

These opening words of the commentary state clearly the religious intentions of the Victorines: their commitment to an apostolic way of life; the need for clear precepts in this regard; the authority of 'the holy fathers' as the guarantee of this commitment; and lastly, with attention to the word 'canon', the explicit link they have forged between the canonical way of life and Augustine himself. The *Exposition* suggests why the Victorines were successful in making Augustine's *Rule* a vital source for reform, for it puts forward a vision of religious living that is authoritative, attractive, and yet demanding.

The *Exposition* is written in a simple yet warm Latin, with a somewhat rambling approach; it comments on Augustine's *Rule* by means of scriptural quotation and recourse to Augustinian themes and citations, with frequent pithy advice, admonition and exhortation. A glance at the commentary shows how successful it was in capturing the monastic spirituality of Augustine and why it was copied and reprinted abundantly throughout subsequent centuries as a guide to living Augustine's *Rule* authentically. While the exposition can, on a surface level, be read as inner directed, serving the institutional needs of this community, Zinn has noted the wider implications of the Victorines' intentions embodied therein: they saw themselves as leading the way in a 'movement to renew the life of cloistered religious discipline under the aegis of the Rule of St Augustine'.[13] Victorine interiority, as learned from Augustine, both spawned and nourished the apostolic life (*vita apostolica*).

Unity and Concord

> It is fitting that we who are bodily gathered together into one, likewise dwell together spiritually. It is of no benefit to us if a single dwelling houses us but a divided will separates us. God pays more attention to a unity of soul than a unity of place. Behold, we are many men in one dwelling, differing life-styles, differing hearts, differing souls. All of these things must be joined together into oneness, one intention and one love directed to God. (*Exposition*, 882)

These comments come early in the *Exposition* and set the stage for a persistent attention throughout to what is necessary for attaining and maintaining true oneness in community, the ultimate goal of the abundant practical admonitions expressed in Augustine's *Rule*.

> Neither our fasting nor our prayers please God unless they be done in harmony. (883)

All the traditional monastic observances, even those deemed most personal, are viewed not simply from a private perspective of personal holiness but from a communal vision of shared holiness. Harmony witnesses to holiness. However, the author makes it clear that to reconcile diversity and difference within this community is a task which implicitly acknowledges that variation must be respected. The goal, as such, is not simply a well-ordered community but one where its dynamism and directionality come from a God-centred love, with God's indwelling Spirit harmonising diverse forms of faithful observance into a harmonious holiness.

> We mutually honor God in each other if we love one another because of God, if we guard his precepts carefully, and become his holy temple by the indwelling of his Spirit in us. (890)

In that sense it can be said that the author, true to the spirit of Augustine, reduces, or better, elevates all monastic virtues to love:

> Indeed, poverty and humility generate love. Love, to be sure, nourishes unity; unity and concord, to be sure, make us into the temple of God. (890–1)

There is no individualised spirituality here, but a shared holiness and love, so that even chastity finds its foundation in love.

> It is exceedingly necessary to mutually guard *our* modesty [italics mine] with vigilance, for if *we* lose it, *we* have lost everything, including *ourselves*. Anyone who loses modesty, loses their soul, loses God, loses himself. But it is for this very reason that *we* live in oneness, so *that we may protect one another*, correct one another, instruct one another; and whatever someone is not able to do by himself, can be done *through the other*. (901)

I have deliberately highlighted the communal emphasis in this exhortation to chastity, for it manifests a profound, God-centred mutuality even in the pursuit of what are seemingly the most intimate dimensions of the holiness called for by the Augustinian *Rule*. Chastity provides a fertile ground for common life and church mission to blossom.

From Exteriority to Interiority

> First we are commanded to abandon our possessions, then not to seek that which is earthly, so that, as a result, we may be freer to yearn for that which is heavenly. (886)

The commentator affirms Augustine's foundational concern that in his community one must move from the external and exterior, the visible and the fleshy, to that which is spiritual, interior and of God. For the author of the *Exposition*, this means an ever-deepening attention to matters of the heart and will.

> We are first drawn towards God by our heart and our will. (884)

There is little doubt that the commentator is echoing a theme that is close to Augustine's deepest insights regarding how God works within us. Augustine himself never tires of insisting that God draws us by 'attracting' us interiorly, working upon our hearts and moving our wills by inner stimulus and interior delights (see for example *Io. eu. tr.* 26.4). Drawing upon a classic Augustinian (and Pauline) antithesis, the contrast between the inner and the outer human being (the author uses typically Augustinian language in his Latin to express the antithesis: *exterior/interior*, *foris/intus*), there is a constant call throughout the *Exposition* to attend to the inner or interior human being (*homo interior*), epitomised in the following exhortation: 'It is necessary that our interior self (*interior homo noster*) as an equitable judge preside over ourselves and what we do exteriorly' (896). The very importance given by canonical spirituality to witness (*docere verbo et exemplo*) makes the inner sourcing of this testimony even more critical, yet this concern for interiority is never allowed to move towards the private or individual since it finds its ultimate fruition in apostolic service. In another passage, interiority is highlighted by calling attention to the importance of the Word of God. The commentator expands here upon Augustine's call in the *Rule* for the servants of God to have 'hungry ears', while taking physical nourishment at the community table:

> In the first place we must prepare our heart to hunger for and desire the word of God . . . And just as the soul is better than the body, just so ought nourishment for the soul delight us more than nourishment for the body. Whenever the Sacred Scriptures are read or explained to us, we ought to realize that God is providing us with spiritual food for refreshing our hearts lest we faint on the way. God is strengthening us against the temptations of the devil and the dangers of this world . . . anyone who hides

> the divine word in his own heart, has a life-giving food to defend oneself from sin . . . (894)

The divine word hidden in the heart is strength and perseverance for the embattled soul. It is certainly this constant attention to the heart, to one's inner intention and interior condition, that draws the commentator ever closer to Augustine's own intense explorations of the inner self that we have already seen in Chapter 1: 'It doesn't matter if we've relinquished our things, if we haven't relinquished our self (*non prodest nobis nostra relinquere, nisi relinquamus et nos*)' (889). All of this means that one must be an astute and honest observer of the self, especially since, as the anonymous commentator insists, the devil is also an equally clever observer of the human heart: 'Our crafty enemy knows everybody's morals and qualities, and even discerns affections. In each one he tempts where he has the best chance of prevailing. Cautious and vigilant is what we must be against such a crafty enemy' (907). Knowing the shrewd craftiness of the enemy, that he is a master of deceit, the servant of God has even greater reason to practise the utmost vigilance over the self. Discernment is thus essential to this Victorine living of the Augustinian *Rule*:

> Behold, it is for this reason that someone ought not to obey their intense desires (*cupiditas*) because it is often the case that such desires deceive, leading us to think something is good when it is in fact harmful. Thus bad desire (*mala cupiditas*) misleads, posturing itself as good when, in fact, it is evil and destructive . . . (909)

The interiority called for here is indeed a discerning interiority, where great attention is given to an inner watchfulness marked by attentive judgement. This admonition is then connected to the *Rule*'s attention to providing books for the members of the community, explicitly identified now as sources for real learning in holiness: 'The servant of God ought to read often. *Lectio divina* is extremely useful for through it we learn what to avoid, what to do, where to direct ourselves' (912).

Study is thus integrated into a practice of interiority, as an important source of self-knowledge and direction. The Victorines, with their deep commitment to study and learning, certainly found in this dimension of Augustine's *Rule* an important affirmation of their way of life and their formal links to Augustine's monastic vision.

The emphasis on interiority finds a further echo in the commentator's reminder that the superior of the community is to be a physician of souls (*medicus animarum*). His office is thus seen as interiorly directed, with a need to maintain a medicine chest of virtues (*medicamenta virtutum*) suitable for remedying the inner maladies of the servants of God of this community (922). The office of superior as envisioned here remains true to Augustine's insistence in the *Rule* that the one in charge must manifest a loving and delicate commitment to attend to the intricate relationship between individual hearts and the life of the community as a whole.

A Shared Grace

Throughout the *Exposition* its author never loses sight of Augustine's medieval title as 'Doctor of Grace' (*Doctor Gratiae*). These servants of God must not forget the 'grace they have in common – *communis gratia*' (see 886). There is an explicit awareness of the need for these Augustinian Canons to be true to the theological foundations upon which the *Rule* was written: 'Ours it is to honor God, God's it is to dwell within and enlighten us through grace' (889). The emphasis on observance, a charged priority during this century and every age of reform, must never lose sight of the only authentic source of that observance, something that even the devil, as the commentator strikingly notes, is well aware of and seeks to undermine (892). This attention to grace suggests that the *Exposition*'s author has studied and meditated upon a variety of well-known Augustinian texts. He notes, for example, the need for the grace of continence, offering an admonition with an affinity to *Confessions* 10.29.40.

> And since our mutual vigilance is not from us but from God, the *Rule* rightly adds: 'God who dwells within you will in this way watch over you through one another.' For our own vigilance for you is insufficient unless God's vigilance be present. Whence Scripture says: 'Unless God keep vigil . . .' (Psalm 126:1). No one can keep pure by depending upon themselves or one's neighbor, except through God. But if God dwells in us, we can do through him what we cannot in ourselves. Let us thus strive to live so that we deign to live in him, he in us, so that through him we may be just and chaste . . . (901)

The author echoes Augustine's sensitive and insistent awareness that there is a mysterious interpenetrating dynamism between self, God, community and grace. Thus, 'through the grace of God' (905), the holiness which is the intent of the *Rule* is always seen as a gifted reality, strikingly called by the author 'the grace of common life – *gratia vitae socialis*' (915). He has coined an expression that reflects the unique communally shared and expressed holiness that lies at the foundations of the Augustinian *Rule* and finds its fullest expression in freedom and love (923).

Apostolic and Canonical

As representative of a significant moment in the history of the Augustinian tradition, the Victorines clearly move within the spirit of Augustine, yet go beyond their patron. The author of the *Exposition* has left his Victorine imprint upon this reading of the Augustinian *Rule* in his 'canonical' understanding of the apostolic nature of their life together: the authority of such a life, the pastoral intent it fulfils. As already stated, both these elements were an integral part of the twelfth-century reform programme undertaken by the canonical movement. One finds throughout the *Exposition* a continuing insistence that the life of this community is intended to 'teach' others, but the commentator first grounds this in the authority of the early church whose ideals Augustine sought to embody.

> [Augustine] strengthens his own comments with apostolic authority . . . (885)
>
> This is what the brothers of the primitive church did. (896)
>
> We live deeply united (*unanimiter*) if we have one soul in God, according to the practice of the primitive church who were one in heart and soul. (889)

The strength of the canonical reform was supported and protected by the authenticity and authority of its ideals – they are the values of the apostolic community. This emphasis served a deeper end, not only ensuring that their witness would never lose sight of its wider benefit for the whole church, but also defending them against possible charges that their reform was novel and so ephemeral. Their life, they could insist, was nothing more than a return to the most ancient and inspired Christian observance. Once again it is this explicit attention to the exemplary or didactic nature of their way of life that stands out and most marks this commentary as 'canonical' in its scope.

> . . . lest we give scandal by our way of life. (893)
>
> It is indeed unbecoming if we live in a reprehensible way, we who must demonstrate to others (*aliis demonstrare*) a manner of right living. (893)
>
> . . . we whom it behoves to live rightly and to demonstrate good example to others (*aliis demonstrare*) . . . (904)
>
> Through *lectio divina* you learn how you ought to live and how you ought to teach others (*alios doceatis*). (912)

Caroline Walker Bynum, it has been noted, has argued that 'to teach by word and example – *docere verbo et exemplo*' is what is distinctive and original about canonical spirituality, which saw its way of life as having a public, ministerial, teaching and ecclesial goal. This commentary does indeed verify her insight:

> Thus canons must live so that no one may justly criticize them. It is indeed incongruous for them to live in a reprehensible way, whose very nature *demands* [italics mine] that they show a way of holiness to others . . . for a good life is necessary for us, is done on our own behalf (*propter nos*), a good reputation however is done for the sake of others (*propter alios*) . . . (898)

'For the sake of others', an apostolic spirituality aware of 'the other' – this is the striking legacy of this medieval exposition of the Augustinian *Rule*. Although the author of this commentary remains unknown, his knowledge of Augustine and the tradition, his wisdom in offering discerning counsel, and his fervour in a dedicated holiness remain anything but hidden: 'I confess that I am ashamed of precious garments. Such are not worthy of this profession, nor of these comments I am making, nor this body, nor these gray hairs' (897). Our anonymous author has made his own Augustine's insistence on love, a love which can never remain closed or hidden, a love which was at the heart of Augustine's deepest religious aspirations: ' . . . for nothing can please God without love. In everything we do it is necessary that love prevail, since love is the mother of virtues, the very root of everything that is good. This is the higher way which leads to heaven' (906).

CONCLUSION

Robert Crouse has noted that '[i]n the intellectual and spiritual life of Europe in the Middle Ages, the influence of St Augustine was all-pervasive.'[14] Augustine was 'the *magister* par excellence of Christian theology and spirituality in Latin Christendom in the Middle Ages'.[15] However, and this is critical to understanding the Augustinianism of movements such as that of the Victorines, Augustine's 'doctrine was continually reinterpreted, modified and enriched by scholars who drew upon a multiplicity of other sources, as well as upon each one's own particular genius. Thus "Medieval Augustinianism" is not a monolithic doctrine, but a continually developing, exceedingly complex and richly variegated tradition.'[16] The Victorines well exemplify this, as they deliberately allowed Augustine and Augustinian themes to shape their thought and intentions, manifesting a reciprocity that will be found throughout the course of the history of this tradition. They took up Augustine and introduced him into new contexts, placed new demands upon him, incorporated him into new theological methods, and in so doing allowed him to address the concerns and preoccupations of their world, offering it an Augustinian response. Indeed, the Victorines flourished at a time of great creativity when other traditions such as that of Pseudo-Dionysius were also beginning to be rediscovered and revived. Yet, even here, as Crouse insists, these other traditions are read in a way that complements Augustine rather than deviates from him. In that sense he suggests that a fertile spiritual-intellectual movement such as that of the Victorines was part of what he calls 'Augustinianisms', various readings of Augustine that tended to highlight some particular aspect or emphasis which flowed out of his rich and seminal thinking.[17] It was a spiritually and intellectually rich world in which the Victorines first began to flourish, finding in Augustine and his tradition the necessary resources to nourish an age hungry for reform and instruction. It finds eloquent summation in a sermon preached on the Feast of St Augustine, grouped in a collection of medieval sermons attributed to Hugh of St Victor:

> And now, beloved, let us see whether we are offspring of our Blessed Father Augustine (*de semine beati Patris Augustini*), that is to say, imitators of him as we ought to be. Let us ask ourselves whether, after his example, we are lovers of the Word of God, imitating his reading and meditation and study and preaching of that Word, doing so in accordance with the grace we have been given. Let

us ask ourselves whether we are imitating his most honorable way of life, living in a holy manner with all complete effort. If we do so, we are indeed his offspring (*vere semen ejus sumus*), and we will truly contemplate the brilliance of the heavenly Jerusalem with him. Let us pray Jesus Christ our Lord to so grant us this. Amen. (*sermo LXXXIV, in festo sancti Augustini*, PL 177, col. 1169)

4. EXEMPLAR AND RULE OF ALL OUR ACTIONS: AUGUSTINE AND THE HERMITS

In 1357, Jordan of Saxony, a member of the mendicant Order known as the Hermits of St Augustine,[1] finally completed a long-awaited and comprehensive volume on the spiritual ideals that guided his religious community. Above all else, he emphasised the lofty Augustinian character of those ideals.

> Although he was a bishop [our blessed father Augustine] often went aside to his brothers in the wilderness for some recollection, afterward returning to his residence to instruct and govern the clergy and people. Then again he would seize the opportunity and retire to his brothers for a while, as he himself reports in a sermon to the priests in Hippo, the one beginning 'In all your works . . .' With the same spiritual practice in mind he also laid it down for the brothers of his second monastery, which he founded in the garden, that in the monastery they should spend their time in prayer, reading and holy meditation, and that then in their preaching they should pour forth to others what God had given them to understand there. It was certainly in view of this initial constitution of the Order that Holy Mother Church directed the hermit brothers of Saint Augustine toward the cities, as shall be shown below. Thus the alternation which we have described between both ways of life may continue in the Order even now, and any devout brother may lead a hermit life in his cell. By doing and teaching what God has deigned to reveal to him in prayer, reading, meditation, or

> even contemplation, that is, by word and example, he may strive to impart it to others . . . This is what our most blessed father Augustine did, and he ought to be the exemplar and rule (*exemplar et regula*) of all our activities: when not with his brothers in the wilderness he lived with the community in his episcopal monastery. (Jordan of Saxony, *The Life of the Brethren* I.11).[2]

Jordan is both instructing and exhorting his fellow Augustinian Hermits regarding how they are to live faithfully the venerable way of life to which they have been called. For Jordan it is not only an exalted vocation but one that can be clearly traced back to Augustine himself.

> The title which the Church of Rome has solemnly decreed and approved for the Order is this: The Order of Hermit Brothers of Saint Augustine. This is the title which Saint Augustine himself gave them, since in the sermon to the priests at Hippo which begins 'In all your works . . .' he calls them his brothers 'in the wilderness', thus distinguishing them from his brothers 'in the episcopal residence'. Hence they are now called the Hermit Brothers of Saint Augustine. (*Life of the Brethren* I.17)

Nearly ten centuries separate Jordan and his hermit brethren from St Augustine. On what basis can he claim not only that Augustine personally gave the Hermits their name, but even suggest that the saint of Hippo was himself a 'man of the wilderness': 'Augustine the hermit'! Certainly, one of the most original chapters in the history of the Augustinian tradition concerns a thirteenth-century religious Order that succeeded not only in convincing their world (and themselves) that they were directly founded by St Augustine but in the very process managed to recast Augustine into one of their own: Augustine the hermit. It is a uniquely medieval tale, filled with legend and even forgery, and yet in its outcome embodied essential Augustinian ideals that would continue to shape and transform the West. Indeed, it was to be one of these Augustinian 'hermits', Martin Luther, an ardent theologian, intensely devout, initially tenaciously dedicated to the cowl he too was convinced Augustine wore, who in the first decades of the sixteenth century would for ever change the face of Western Christianity. And, as will be seen, the historical claim to Augustine would be ever chastened by the awareness that without exemplary living any hereditary link quickly moves from commendation to condemnation.

The thirteenth century was a time of reform and innovation in Western Christianity. Throughout Europe there were calls for a return to evangelical simplicity, which interestingly coincided with an economic upturn that saw in places like Italy the rapid growth of a middle class and the expansion of cities. Town squares would not only be crowded with booths offering the wares of merchants and traders, but to the noise of the vendors was added the reform-minded voices of wandering preachers. This is the world that gave birth to a St Francis of Assisi and his companions in poverty and to a St Dominic and his band of preachers. While the Franciscans and Dominicans would become the largest and most renowned of the 'new' mendicant (begging) religious Orders,[3] they were not alone. Joining them were the Carmelites, the Servites, various other groups, and the Augustinian Hermits. All of these groups would be marked by a new evangelical fervour, a dedication to popular preaching, and a closeness to the people: their brothers, 'friars', is what they would be popularly called.

In the face of strong resistance and difficult historical circumstance, some far-sighted religious leaders were increasingly aware that the religious ferment of the times, made even more critical by its awakening in the rapidly expanding cities, called for bold yet wise action. In 1215, in the twilight of his long and fruitful reign, Pope Innocent III finally found the ripe moment for calling a universal reforming council, the Fourth Lateran Council. It intended to bring order to a host of religious challenges facing the church at the time. These challenges ranged from the questionable doctrines of emerging religious movements to the widespread moral and spiritual laxity of many clergy and monks. The Council put forward legislative canons to address these issues, including an effort to rein in the unregulated proliferation of religious groups. Arguing that excessive diversity was a source of religious confusion for the faithful, it took the radical step of prohibiting the establishment of any new religious orders. It also decided that any of the recently founded religious communities, if they did not wished to be suppressed, must accept an approved Rule: Basil's, Benedict's, or Augustine's. To this legislation were added other canons regarding the finances and pastoral ministry of religious orders, including their relationship to local bishops. Dominic and his preachers adopted the *Rule of St Augustine*; Francis' evangelical 'experiment' received papal approbation; and efforts were undertaken throughout Italy and Europe to implement the canons of the Fourth Lateran Council.

THE HERMITS OF SAINT AUGUSTINE

As part of this effort at reform and regulation, scattered hermit groups in the region of Tuscany began adopting the *Rule of St Augustine* and uniting into ecclesiastically recognised groupings. At this time the term 'hermit' was a somewhat flexible term used to denote religious men who lived in remote and rural areas; they often began as solitaries but were quickly joined by others. They were very similar to monks in that they lived in buildings similar to monasteries, prayed together and lived lives of poverty, celibacy and asceticism. The term 'hermit', however, distinguished them from the often large, well-established, and sometimes powerful and wealthy monasteries that dominated the European landscape at this time, most often following the *Rule of St Benedict*.[4] Often the designation 'hermit' was chosen as a deliberate rejection of what was seen as 'establishment' religiosity, these 'hermits' seeking something more evangelical, radical and spontaneous, less institutionalised. They were eventually required by church legislation to carry staffs as their distinguishing symbol. They were not to be mistaken for the monks! The presence of these ascetic hermits in secluded areas did not fail to attract the attention of local farmers and shepherds and even inhabitants of not-too-distant towns and cities. Soon the hermitages became centres of pilgrimage, where piety was nourished and spiritual counsel and care were sought. A number of the larger, more organised hermitages began to establish houses in nearby towns and cities. As a result the pilgrims who had sought out the hermits in the wilderness no longer needed to leave their town or city to avail themselves of their pastoral care.

In 1244, under the direction of Pope Innocent IV, representatives of various Tuscan hermits, already in the process of uniting their hermitages into a single religious grouping, gathered in Rome and were formally recognised as the 'Hermit Brothers of Tuscany of the Order of St Augustine'.[5] This title quickly became 'Hermit Brothers of the Order of St Augustine' and, by 1255, in a Bull entitled *His quae pro* of Alexander IV, they are simply referred to as the 'Order of Hermits of St Augustine' (*Ordo Eremitarum sancti Augustini*). In 1256 other hermit groups were united to them and within the next few decades the Order of Hermits of St Augustine grew rapidly, establishing foundations throughout Europe, from England to Hungary to Spain, with the greatest concentration of their houses in Italy. The Augustinian Hermits had taken on their final form and would now begin to make their presence and prestige felt. Balbino Rano, a Spanish Augustinian historian who, perhaps more than any other recent scholar, has sought to unravel this complicated history, notes that from the beginning two characteristics marked these Hermits as a religious community: their structure as an apostolic fraternity and their dedication to Augustine or 'Augustinianness' (Rano, 'Origin and Charism', 224). It is the second characteristic that makes these 'Hermits' an important manifestation of the Augustinian tradition.

The 1357 excerpt from the Augustinian Hermit Jordan of Saxony which introduced this chapter speaks of their direct and explicit foundation by St Augustine. How did such a bold claim come about? What proof was offered for it? What purpose did it serve? It is only modern historical-criticism that has enabled recent scholarship to face this claim, disputed from the outset, discover its genesis and intention, and thus address the question of the Augustinianness of an Order which still today claims the title 'Augustinian'. The answer is not simple and the limits of this volume do not permit a detailed answer. Two factors were unmistakably at work, one internal and one external.

Regarding the external, there was the legislation of the Fourth Lateran Council which proscribed new religious orders. Was this not a new order and so in violation of conciliar legislation? Whisperings in this regard came to a head with the convocation of the Second Council of Lyons in 1274. In its preliminary draft legislation it seemed to call into question the legitimacy of the Augustinian Hermits. The Hermits mustered their greatest thinkers and canonists and survived the challenge. In the process a dossier was developed that demonstrated their direct links to St Augustine.[6] The decree of the Council concerning religious orders, promulgated by Pope Gregory X in 1275, acknowledged that the Augustinian Hermits antedated the decree of Lateran IV but also provided them with an ominous warning:

> . . . we allow them to remain as they are until we shall have decided otherwise. We intend to make provision for them and the other orders, including those that are not mendicant, according to what we believe to be best for the salvation of souls and for their own condition. (Rano, 'Origin and Charism', 214)

'Until we shall have decided otherwise' provided both external threat and creative stimulus to provoke the Augustinian Hermits to better secure their future. Careful textual study of documents of this period reveals a gradual shift in discourse from addressing St Augustine as Father (a title of respect shared by all the religious orders with the *Rule of St*

Augustine) to addressing him as Founder. The claim to that title was supported by legends that alleged that even before Augustine returned to Africa he encountered hermits in Italy (Tuscany, to be specific!). According to these narratives, he lived with them, wore a hermit's habit, and finally, before leaving for Africa, wrote for them a *Rule*. These legends began to spread throughout the Order of the Augustinian Hermits and quickly became 'proof texts'. These were then gathered and published by the Hermits to make public their history. Writing in 1334, Henry of Friemar, an Augustinian scholar and theologian in Erfurt, could thus make the following assertion, set forth in the first formal history of the Order:

> After his baptism Blessed Augustine donned the hermit's habit and remained with Blessed Simplicianus [the priest Simplicianus of the *Confessions*, so instrumental in preparing Augustine for conversion and baptism, has now become a hermit!] near Milan for about a year . . . The fact that Augustine did don and wear the hermit's habit is made clear by Ambrose in his *Sermon on the Baptism and Conversion of Saint Augustine*, in which he says that after he had baptized Augustine the latter donned a black habit with a cincture . . . Since he had found many hermits living a holy life in the solitude of Tuscany, he put in at last to the place of our brothers, known as Centocelle, which is said to have been the first location of our Order, and he remained with those brothers for two years. He also gave them the rule and way of life which he composed as one now well advanced in the disciplines of the faith. This information is derived from *old unabridged legends* [italics mine] . . . That the Order of Hermit Brothers of Saint Augustine and the brothers of this Order are the true and proper sons of Blessed Augustine and that he is truly their father is clear from this, that he wore their habit in a hermitage and gave them a rule of life, as is evident from what was said earlier . . . (Cited by Rano, 'Origin and Charism', 193–5)

Despite the fact that all Henry can bring forward are 'old unabridged legends', he speaks with conviction and certitude regarding the origins of the Augustinian Hermits and their intimate and direct link to St Augustine: Augustine was himself a hermit, dressed as a hermit, and personally gave them the *Rule* that bears his name. While the Hermits were convinced by this line of argumentation and 'proof', others were not and this only increased the Hermits' efforts to validate the claim. The Augustinian Canons, some linked to groups mentioned in Chapter 3, others newly founded, responded vociferously against such declarations. They drew upon their own legends to show that Augustine directly founded them, the Augustinian Canons, and personally wrote his *Rule* for them. The Dominicans and Franciscans were likewise outraged, since the Hermits' claim to an earlier foundation had implications regarding precedence and prestige, and the same was true for the Benedictines. This outcry did not dismay the Augustinian Hermits, who continued to muster all their energies to defend their claims. They were quite successful: in 1327 the Prior General of the Hermits received papal approval for joint custody of the relics of St Augustine in Pavia, south of Milan. This bestowal was final proof of their authenticity, and would become a key argument in subsequent debates, mainly with the Augustinian Canons:

> . . . [As further proof] there are the actions of the most holy Father and Lord Pope John XXII, who at the pious insistence of Father Master William of Cremona, during the first year of the latter's generalate, and with the approval of the sacred college of cardinals, graciously bestowed on our Order, in perpetuity, the care of the site where the venerable body of our most holy father and patron, Blessed Augustine, lies. He confirmed the gift in an authoritative and most obliging privilege, in which he says: 'We have thought it right that the father should be united to his sons, the head to its members, the teacher to his disciples, the captain to the soldiers who devotedly

> do battle under so great a father.' This makes it perfectly clear that holy Mother Church recognizes Augustine as the true father and special head of our Order, and consequently that the brothers of the Order should be called his true sons and authentic members. (Rano, *Augustinian Origins*, 199)

Though never without critics, these bold claims simply passed into received history until the twentieth century when historical-critical scholarship enabled the real historical beginnings of the Augustinian Hermits to surface. Nonetheless, the underlying spiritual dynamics of this thirteenth- and fourteenth-century 'Augustinian' episode reveal much of what was at the heart of medieval spirituality: the importance of the figure of the saint and the prominent place hagiography played in this regard; the weight given to tangible relics which brought one into real contact with a saint's authority and holiness; the concern for proper ancient credentials which functioned as a veritable insurance policy for security, privilege and precedence. All of this found a proper place in a religious world in transition, where spiritual competition was both intense and taken for granted. Of note likewise is how this peculiar episode of Augustinianism highlighted the significance of the person and figure of Augustine as much as his thought and writings, another indication of the weight behind his name throughout the medieval era. Nonetheless, a text of Augustine did emerge with particular importance in these events, his *Rule* being viewed by the Hermits as the saint's personal legacy to them. The final product of this was a vibrant and direct spiritual relationship between the Hermits and Augustine with its own distinctive approach to Augustinian spirituality. Its first mature fruit was Jordan of Saxony's 1357 *Life of the Brethren* (*Liber Vitasfratrum*).

The Life of the Brethren

There is no doubt that Jordan's *Life of the Brethren* sought to verify the Hermits' ties to Augustine. Yet even more importantly it sought to call the Augustinian Hermits themselves to a faithful living out of the impressive legacy that was identified with their saintly bishop and founder. Accordingly, if their claims of origin were in response to external pressures placed upon the Order, Jordan's lucid articulation of an Augustinian spirituality implies that internally the Order had a felt need for a clear spiritual identity and authentic standard of holiness. The two principal 'unions' that legally constituted the Order, those of 1244 and 1256, meant that different religious communities, each with a unique history, tradition and experience, were now forced to forge a single identity. There is clear evidence that this 'forging' was challenged by a reluctance to abandon cherished local practices, even to the point of resisting a uniform religious habit to be worn. It is no doubt difficult for many moderns to appreciate the importance of the religious habit for proper identification during this period. It served in many ways as the equivalent of a trademark. Depending upon this particular and recognisable label, donations were given, doors were opened or shut, pulpits were made available or not.

There were further points of contention. Since the Hermits were officially numbered among the mendicant orders, religious communities that lived off begging and not from fixed-incomes (a practice that coincided with their presence in the cities where begging was practical and effective), what were they to do about the remote hermitages that remained? Could they be allowed to maintain income-producing property since in scantily populated areas begging was not possible? The form of the religious habit and the practice of poverty were just two of many identity issues that the Order of Hermits had to face in order to survive and flourish. And if they claimed to be 'Hermits of St Augustine', the answer to these and other identity questions would have to be staked out in Augustinian terms. Jordan does just that in his *Life of the Brethren.*

> In his plan to renew the apostolic life, the founder of our Order and its most blessed father Augustine based his whole approach on these words [he has just cited Acts 4:32, 34]. Thus at the start of his second sermon on the common life of clerics, where he wishes to explain the fundamental teaching of his *Rule* to those who profess it, he has the deacon Lazarus read this very passage of scripture, and then he reads it himself, adding these words: 'You have heard what we desire: pray that we may be able to accomplish it' (*s.* 356.1). By carefully examining the mind of Augustine as expressed in his *Rule* and in the sermons which he gave on the common life of clerics, as well as in his other words of advice, we discover that he built his Order completely on the foundation of community or, better, communion. (*Life of the Brethren* I.2)

Thus, moving beyond the legendary claims, Jordan successfully plumbs the core and underpinnings of Augustine's distinctive monastic vision. He continues:

> This communion is fourfold. The *first communion* [italics mine] involved living together in the same place. We read of this in one of the psalms: 'Behold how good and how pleasant it is for brothers to live in unity' (*Ps.* 132:1) . . . the apostles and the other believers to whom these words apply followed them literally, living together in a common house. The *second communion* consists in oneness of spirit. This occurs when men lead a common life, being of one heart and one soul, and of one manner, that is, of one observance . . . The *third communion* is one of temporal possessions, and this comes about when no one has any temporal goods as his own, but all things are possessed in common . . . The *fourth communion* involves proportional distribution, that is, when each one receives in proportion to his needs . . . (*Life of the Brethren* I.2)

Jordan used this fourfold scheme of community and communion as the organising principle of his *Life of the Brethren*.

With this guiding framework he sought to rise above the disputes and claims about spiritual pedigree and provide a helpful manual of practical advice and spiritual ideals for living the Augustinian life. Jordan drew upon the wisdom of desert monasticism, the writings of John Cassian, and a developing lore within the Order, placing it in dialogue with the writings of Augustine (including a number of pseudo-Augustinian writings). Homely advice merges with anecdotal lessons. The hermit life ought not to be undertaken prematurely: 'It is clear that the anchorites enjoy a higher and more perfect state, but before they undertake their life of seclusion they must first have been tried in the crucible of common life (*in coenobiis praeexercitatos*)' (I.4). Jordan supports this with an anecdote:

> There was a brother who made an insistent request of his prior provincial for permission to change over to a certain solitary place and there to serve the Lord. The provincial made a wise examination of his motivation, taking into account his former manner of life, which he knew to be excellent: he had never fallen under censure in any community. Yet he discerned that his request did not come from the inspiration of the Holy Spirit but from a desire for harmful peace and false freedom. If a man has never learned to live at peace in a monastery with his brothers nor to obey the advice of his superiors, and then seeks to go to a place of solitude, what else can such a man be after if not to throw off the toilsome yoke of obedience to the observances of the monastery and to live just as he pleases in a place where no one can correct him? Thus the provincial wisely refused what this brother had unwisely sought. (I.8)

Jordan also expends much effort in explaining and defending the observance of poverty by the mendicant Augustinian Hermits. He draws upon Augustine's *Sermons* 355–6, the *Praeceptum*'s exhortations to common possession of all things, and the example of Augustine himself. Once again he offers both exhortation and anecdote.

> It is of little value for us to strip ourselves of temporal things on our entry into religion if we do not maintain ourselves in this state of nakedness throughout the course of our lives. Therefore not only is it necessary for a brother to renounce everything in accordance with the evangelical rule, but he must also endeavor to live in poverty according to that same rule, or at least according to the apostolic rule, on which the *Rule of Saint Augustine* is founded, as has been said. (IV.12)

He follows this admonition with a more ominous story, indicative of the struggles posed by the call to common life and poverty.

> I knew another brother who used to embezzle for himself some of what was due to the community. He was healthy and fit, but one day when he had come back to the monastery from the city, where he had eaten, he was found sitting in the bathroom, dead. (IV.15)

> I have experience of a similar example in another brother who labored under the same vice and received a similar end in the bathroom. See how the followers of Judas were fated to end their lives in a shameful place during a base act, as if with their entrails poured out! (IV.15)

Behind such extreme examples is an underlying urgent concern for an Augustinian spirituality which is utterly communal in its scope and practice. Both unfortunates perished because they took for themselves 'what was due to the community'!

Throughout the entire work Jordan provides 'the brethren' with challenging material for their personal spiritual reflection and return to the ideals, calling them repeatedly to see themselves as true 'sons of Augustine' and so live. Thus, in the last analysis, he admits that 'authenticity' is not really supported by historical claims but only by faithful observance.

> If any of the Orders that follow the *Rule of Saint Augustine*

> wished to debate over which of them had the principal claim on the *Rule*, that is, which had received it first or especially or most worthily, thus seeking thereby to gain the greater privilege, I would say without any reserve that it is they who most devoutly and fervently follow what it contains that can glory most worthily in a special claim to it. If I had my way this is how our sacred Order would lay claim to the *Rule*, more than by the fact that it was to our fathers that Augustine first gave it: for we should not bother with who was first to receive it, but with who is best in observing it. (II.14)

It is no wonder that Jordan's work was to become the standard spiritual text for the Order for many subsequent centuries.

THE AUGUSTINIAN SCHOOL

Throughout the Middle Ages theology was virtually synonymous with the name Augustine,[7] and from this theology spiritual practice was born. The religious experience that flowed out of this spiritual practice in turn led to the need to better understand and give voice to the experience. Theology deepened and developed. Though recent centuries tended to separate theology and spiritual practice, the efforts of the Augustinian Hermits to gain recognition as true sons and heirs of the Bishop of Hippo resulted not only in the legends we have just seen but likewise in an abundance of exegetical and theological writings imbued with the spirituality of Augustine to such a degree that one author speaks of this period as 'the late medieval Augustinian renaissance' (Saak, 'Augustine in the Later Middle Ages', 368). These writings have been and continue to be the subject of much scrutiny, analysis and debate, with some scholars noting sufficient commonality and shared characteristics among them to be able to speak of an 'Augustinian School'.[8] Only after a brief consideration of some traits these writings share will it be possible to address the question of a 'school'.

In the first place, these works give Scripture place of prominence. The originating Constitutions of the Augustinian Hermits, the 1290 *Ratisbon Constitutions*,[9] direct that novices entering the community be initiated into the Scriptures: 'so that he may read Holy Scripture avidly, listen to it devotedly, and learn it ardently – *ut sanctam Scripturam avide legat, devote audiat et ardenter addiscat*' (18.113). It is clear that the Bible was intended to have an important role in the spiritual formation of the Augustinian Hermits and it has been suggested that this in turn found root in the spiritual writings of the Augustinian School. For example, Jordan of Saxony proposes the example of Augustine as model in this regard: 'We read of Saint Augustine also that if not at prayer or caring for the needs of the church, day and night he would devote himself to the study of the scriptures and sacred writings' (*Life of the Brethren* II.22). He preceded this comment with an exhortation from Augustine regarding the study of Scripture, from a pseudo-sermon, 'To the Brethren in the Wilderness':

> My brothers [he quotes from the sermon] read the sacred scriptures, and there you will find clearly what you should seek after and what you should avoid . . . they above all invite us to love God: they enlighten our hearts, purify our tongues, test our consciences, sanctify our souls, strengthen our faith, repel the devil, ward off sin, and bring heat to souls that are cold; they bring in the light of knowledge and cast out the shadows of ignorance, they extinguish the sadness of the world and light up the joy of the Holy Spirit, giving the thirsty to drink. (*Life of the Brethren* II.22)

Although these were not his authentic words, Augustine would not disagree with their intention: here the personal study of Scripture is linked with a personal holiness of life. Apparently, the exhortation was heeded. There are abundant scriptural commentaries left by members of the Augustinian Hermits, though many still remain unstudied (see Saak, 'Augustine in the Later Middle Ages', 370).

This emphasis on Scripture was accompanied by a second characteristic, the reading and study of Augustine. It is evident that its leading thinkers made the move away from what has been called 'happy quoting', the medieval penchant for going to collections of extracts, grouped under various topics, so that one never really engaged the author in context (Saak, 'Augustine in the Later Middle Ages', 379). A study of medieval library catalogues from the houses of the Augustinian Hermits reveals a remarkable abundance of Augustine's writings there,[10] indicating that the actual works of Augustine were collected and, one must suppose, actually read. The greatest monument to this is the *Milleloquium Sancti Augustini* of Bartholomew of Urbino, a member of the Augustinian Hermits who completed the work *c.*1345. It became one of the most important medieval Augustinian works and was intended as a reading guide to the thought and writings of Augustine. It was the product of an actual reading and study of Augustine's works, saw many reprints, and even today is a valuable tool for those who study the Augustinian manuscript tradition. Thus the Augustinian School can be said to have employed a pioneering historico-critical method that relied on reading actual texts in their original setting, enabling its writers to cite Augustine abundantly and from a wide range of his works.

Regarding the content of the teaching of the Augustinian School, there was a prominent Christocentrism, that could take the form of an extended meditation on Christ's life and passion,[11] or manifest itself in the affirmation of Giles of Rome, the leading voice of Augustinian writers (*c.*1245–1316), that 'there can only be true justice in that state whose founder and leader is Christ' (Zumkeller, 91). James of Viterbo (*c.*1255–1308), successor to Giles in the Order's chair of theology in Paris, wrote the *De regimine christiano*, 'the oldest independent treatise on the Church' (Zumkeller, 29), emblematic of the deep ecclesial concern of these Augustinian writers. There was, not surprisingly, a strong anti-Pelagianism among them, complemented positively by an emphasis on Augustine's theology of grace. Gregory of Rimini (d. 1358) is the most prominent theologian of grace in this regard.

As early as 1287 the General Chapter of the Augustinian Hermits sought to ensure that their professors or *magistri* employed a uniform approach to teaching and so ordered that the thought of Giles of Rome was to be studied and observed throughout the Order. This legislation, continued in the 1290 *Constitutions*, seemed to have been understood broadly rather than narrowly. Thus it is perhaps best not to look for the identity of an 'Augustinian School' in a rigid set of particular methods and defined doctrines. Adolar Zumkeller OSA, a German scholar who has written extensively on the Augustinian School, sums up its contours in this way:

> . . . we can find this independent Augustinianism of the late medieval Augustinian school characterized – somewhat schematically – by a double factor, the primacy of love and that of grace. The *primacy of love* is demonstrated in the theories of the priority of the good over the true and the will over the intellect, in the concept of '*caritas*' as the highest goal of theology and its characterization as affective knowledge, as well as in the teachings that God as '*glorificator*' is the proper subject of theology and that the essence of salvation consists more in an act of the will than of the intellect [one could say an act of love rather than of knowledge], finally also in the role accorded to love in the economy of grace, insofar as it moves the will not physically but morally '*per amorem alliciendo*'. (Zumkeller, 27)

Perhaps no Augustinian thinker sums this up better than Giles of Rome in his insistence that 'the first end of theology is love' (Zumkeller, 20, 23). It is precisely because of this emphasis on love which in turn shaped its understanding of grace that the Augustinian School can be understood to have integrated theology and spirituality into a singular vision of the Christian life. This affective assertion of the primacy of love and grace did not remain within the confines of the theological lecture hall. It took the form of great art that filled medieval churches with images of Augustine the Bishop in hermit habit, intently meditating and pondering the mystery of God; it inspired dialogue with an emerging humanism, creating centres like that in Florence where figures like Petrarch could find refuge and come to refer to Augustine as *gloriossimus Pater* (Saak, 'Augustine in the Later Middle Ages', 371); it led to Augustinian Confraternities where Augustine was not only read but his *Rule* was taken as a guide for life in the world. It certainly added to the ferment and intensity of calls for reform and renewal throughout the period, Augustine offering both orthodox anchor and provocative discourse for such calls. Finally it found eloquent and prophetic expression in preaching, the Augustinian churches in Europe assuming an architecture that provided for grand scale 'preaching events' where huge numbers of faithful could gather and listen. It ought to come as no surprise that this Augustinianism will spark even more radical calls for renewal, as we shall see in the next chapter.

CONCLUSION

Augustine was certainly never quite as the Augustinian Hermits portrayed him, yet his love for Scripture, his insistence upon community, his way of understanding faith, his dedication to the church, and his untiring ministry to others was taken up by the Hermits in a way that genuinely linked them to their adopted father. Perhaps more than anything else, they succeeded in giving Augustine's *Rule* a place of prominence in Christian spirituality, placing it at the heart of their religious observance – something that continues to this day.

In 1969, after some seven hundred years of history, the Augustinian Hermits formally requested papal permission to call themselves simply 'the Augustinians', the 'Order of St Augustine'.[12] If this freed them from the weight of medieval legends it also burdened them with greater responsibility to keep alive Jordan of Saxony's already-noted admonition:

> If any of the Orders that follow the *Rule of Saint Augustine* wished to debate over which of them had the principal claim on the *Rule*, that is, which had received it first or especially or most worthily, thus seeking thereby to gain the greater privilege, I would say without any reserve that it is they who most devoutly and fervently follow what it contains that can glory most worthily in a special claim to it. If I had my way this is how our sacred Order would lay claim to the *Rule*, more than by the fact that it was to our fathers that Augustine first gave it: for we should not bother with who was first to receive it, but with who is best in observing it. (*Life of the Brethren* II.14)

5. A THEOLOGICAL LIFE: A SPIRITUALITY FOR REFORMERS

> If you want to be seen as really Augustinian you should imitate his study and his life. If Augustine were alive he would be quicker to recognize me than to recognize many who pride themselves in the most stupid way on his name. (Erasmus writing to Canon Martin Lipsius)[1]

To enter into the religious history of the sixteenth century, a century that irrevocably transformed the face of Western Christianity, is to embark upon no easy task.[2] It was a time of religious ferment where mutually incomprehensible spiritual world-views found themselves on a collision course. The quantity of literature and the still-raging questions about the nature and consequences of the Protestant Reformation and the Roman Catholic Counter-Reformation offer resources that make a full and accurate assessment of this time of radical change and often bitter spiritual conflict surely impossible in a work such as this. The upheavals of this century demonstrate more than any other that spirituality can never be limited to considerations of piety and practices, separated from their deepest theological wellsprings.

But the subject of this chapter is clear: the place and impact of Augustine and the tradition associated with his name upon this century of reform and counter-reform. Augustine's complex richness will clearly manifest conflicting receptions during these pivotal decades. Further, and perhaps as in no other era, these manifestations of the spirituality of Augustine will find themselves embedded in complex theological-ecclesiological questions, as well as broader questions of cultural, social and political history. As the century began, a mounting reaction against Scholastic theology was well under way: it was perceived by many to be too philosophical and too far removed from an experience of faith rooted in Scripture, liturgy and prayer. As the century progresses, new theological models will be proposed that will generate heated exchange. At the same time, Western Europe found itself sorely scarred, with enormous religious, historical and political consequences, by the divisions resulting from the Avignon papacy and the Western Schism, even further challenged by a rising sense of nationalism. Culturally speaking, the Renaissance and a new humanism were on the rise; their manifestations could be blatantly pagan or overtly religious, the latter evident in a desire to return to originating Christianity and its authentic texts. And then there was the papacy: able to wield enormous political, military and economic power; perceived by its critics as incapable of exercising real spiritual or moral authority. It is not surprising that once again, in this time of unrest and transition, the spiritual authority of Augustine of Hippo would be used as a rallying point for radically opposed responses. His voluminous writings, many of which confronted ancient conflicts, were read anew to provide a wealth of theological analyses and penetrating critiques that will be used to address a Christianity likewise in conflict.

To appreciate the varied receptions that the Augustinian tradition received during this century, four representative figures will be considered. Each read Augustine from a unique perspective. Some described themselves as 'Augustinian', others were so designated by subsequent history. Viewed together they manifest the competing forms that Augustinianism took in the sixteenth century. The figures are: the Christian humanist, Desiderius Erasmus; the German 'prophet', Martin Luther; the Genevan reformer, John Calvin; and the Prior General of the Augustinian Hermits and Papal Legate at the Council of Trent, Jerome Seripando. Each of them had a unique intellectual/spiritual development in relationship to Augustine, each came to a firm position regarding what he considered to be the essence of his thought, each found in him an authoritative voice for addressing the spiritual crises engulfing Western Europe, and each found in him a way to respond to critics. In sketching their portraits and placing them side by side, we will see that a remarkably diverse Augustine emerges; at the conclusion of this chapter this diversity will require some attention.

DESIDERIUS ERASMUS (1466?–1536)

Anyone acquainted with Erasmus as the brilliant and mordant humanist of Rotterdam may be surprised to see him leading this list of sixteenth-century 'Augustinian reformers'. He is well known for his oft-repeated and seemingly anti-Augustinian quip: 'In one single page of Origen I will learn more about Christian philosophy than from ten pages of Augustine' (Letter to Jean Eck, May 1518).[3] This, however, was not Erasmus's final word on Augustine. What is most important to note about his appreciation of Augustine is that it saw much development, particularly in the latter part of his life. Erasmus's story is that of a humanist who progressively distanced himself from its more secular forms, turning to a humanism ever more infused with and conformed to Christian piety. It was specifically during this late transformation that Augustine began to exercise an increasingly more profound influence upon the heart of this man of letters, a development marked by distinct stages.

Erasmus had first gained notoriety by the brilliance and eloquence with which he lent his voice and pen to the humanistic renaissance under way upon the European continent. Among many other things, it was a movement intent upon the recovery, if not rediscovery, of a highly regarded past. Accordingly, humanists such as Erasmus took special interest in ancient languages and literature: the study of the Greek and Latin classics and the Hebrew Bible found prominent place in the humanist curriculum. When Erasmus thus joined the monastery of Augustinian Canons at Steyn in 1487 his motivation seems to have been as much intellectual as it was religious. There he hoped to find a setting for 'study and fellowship',[4] as his writings of the period speak of this monastic 'retreat' in terms more classical than religious-biblical. Like the young Augustine before his conversion, Erasmus sincerely yearned to be part of 'a community of scholars sheltered from worldly concerns' (Kaufman, 114), reminiscent of the yearnings of a young Augustine 'before conversion'. But this was not to be; he found himself frustrated by various controversies that engaged him both within and outside the monastery.

Throughout this period Jerome continued to be Erasmus's preferred author, but change was under way. He managed to secure an appointment as secretary to the Bishop of Cambrai, an opportunity to leave the monastery gracefully. In this new capacity he continued to devote himself to his studies and an encounter with the *De doctrina Christiana* in 1494 effected a change in his assessment of Augustine. While he still preferred Jerome's style, finding the African bishop to be wordy and obscure, it was his perception of Augustine's endorsement of pagan culture in the *De doctrina Christiana* (2.40.60) that prompted a change in Erasmus. In the passage Augustine draws upon a patristic commonplace based upon Exodus 3:22; 11:2–3; 12:35–36: just as the Israelites rightfully 'despoiled the Egyptians' of their gold and jewellery for use in the promised land, so might the Christian thinker 'despoil' pagan culture of its gold and jewellery, the riches of its learning, for use in the new promised land that was Christian culture. His admiration of the *De doctrina Christiana* shifted Erasmus's interests beyond Jerome, a 'master of style', to an Augustine now viewed as an authoritative 'master of argument'. He thus drew heavily upon Augustine's work for his *Liber Apologeticus*, a defence of humanism with, ironically, a virtually Pelagian approach to the merits of human effort in this regard (Kaufman, 120). At this time, however, Erasmus was not a dedicated student of the Fathers, interested in plumbing the depth of their thought; rather, he was looking for an authority to legitimate his personal dedication to classical study. In fact, at this time in his life he showed very little theological interest in Augustine, using him principally as a powerful ally in his war against 'the Barbarians', those who rejected any Christian rapprochement with ancient culture. Béné, a leading Erasmus scholar, calls this initial encounter with Augustine the first great moment in what he sees as a four-stage development of an 'Augustinian Erasmus' (Béné, 1969, 428).

Erasmus now found himself increasingly swept into the by now widespread efforts for church reform and renewal of piety and began to understand that this meant, above all, a renewal of theology. He had a lasting effect on the practice of Christian life in this century with the publication of his little work entitled *Enchiridion Militis Christiani*, where he offers 'a theology of the Christian life'. While this work has often been seen as one where Augustine plays little part, the work of Béné has forced a reconsideration of this assessment by demonstrating clearly that the humanist used the *De doctrina Christiana* as both model and sourcebook for the 'theological life' he lays out here. Supported by the authority of Augustine he proposes that classical authors, read carefully, prepare one's spirit to take up the Scriptures; he lays out a Platonism, close to that of Augustine's, as the way to prepare one's spirit for the same task; he quotes Augustine to insist that Scripture must be taken up with 'the greatest purity of soul' (*doct. chr.* 1.10.10), with a similar Augustinian emphasis on the virtue of humility. With this programme 'one comes to the hidden treasures of eternal wisdom' (*Enchiridion* 22–3, Béné, 1969, 146ff.). Once again this final statement is based on Augustine (*doct. chr.* 2.41.62). Thus while the surface appeal in the *Enchiridion* is to Plato, its underlying authority is Augustine, an 'Augustinian inspired' Platonism (Béné, 1969, 150). Likewise, his *Twenty-two Rules*, a guide to the 'new piety' laid out in Chapter VIII of the *Enchiridion*, as well as the conclusion of the work, show Augustinian influence (Béné, 1969, 162). This was not disputational theology but was intended to serve as a handbook 'for a theological life – *ad vitam theologicam*', a new piety, a new 'theological spirituality' (Kaufman, 121).

The mountain of tomes of Scholastic theology, Erasmus declares, offers little teaching for what he sees as the real Christian task: 'to live well – *ad recte vivendum*' (Kaufman, 121). What is significant here, Béné notes, is the important role played by Augustinian sources in this first manifestation of what he calls '*piété érasmienne* – Erasmian piety' (Béné, 1969, 181), a piety permeated with humanism, but now employed 'to embellish the Lord's temple' (see *doct. chr.* 22.40.61). This work signals Erasmus's next phase, totally dedicated to exegetical endeavours.

In the *Enchiridion* Erasmus laid out a programme that would lead to an informed yet religious reading of Scripture (in this he shares much in common with reformers like Luther and Calvin). The results were seen to be not merely speculative for Erasmus as, like Augustine, he decided to 'consecrate the rest of his life to the word of God' (Béné, 1969, 197). Béné describes this change as the '*l'orientation nouvelle de l'augustinisme d'Erasme*'. One of the fruits of this new commitment was an original Latin translation of the Greek New Testament, a project which flowed from the humanistic piety inspired by Augustine's *De doctrina Christiana*. There he found Augustine insisting upon the importance of knowing the Bible in its original language, that the exegete should draw upon wider knowledge when necessary, that Scripture is rhetorically powerful, and that piety is as important as intelligence for true biblical understanding. Erasmus will echo these Augustinian precepts in his *Preface* to the New Testament, his *Methodus*, and his *Ratio Verae Theologiae*. While departing from Augustine in some details, Erasmus's exegetical programme is deliberately Augustinian, not simply in broad outline but even in 'the particulars of Augustine's thought' (Béné, 277–9). For example, Erasmus takes up Augustine's call to exercise moderation and discretion in matters exegetical: 'sober and thoughtful judgement – *sed eas sobrie diligenterque dijudicent*' and 'restraint – *ne quid nimis*' are necessary virtues for one who would interpret the Bible (see *doct. chr.* 2.39.58). Thus with Augustine's support, Erasmus proposes prudence as an essential quality for the biblical theologian, a disposition he found lacking in Luther (Béné, 1969, 270, 280).

The final phase of Erasmus's Augustinian development is well represented by his *Ecclesiastes*, a manual for Christian preachers. This work sums up many of his later writings in what it offers: a distinct programme for a life of study and devotion at the service of a Christian culture, envisioned here through the office of the preacher. Not surprisingly, he turns once again to the *De doctrina Christiana*, drawing from it three specific emphases. First, echoing Augustine, he insists upon the importance of the moral and spiritual qualities of the preacher, complemented predictably by a sound liberal education; second, he lays out a thoroughly Augustinian method for understanding and unravelling the obscurity of Scripture; finally, he calls upon Augustine to support his emphasis on the preacher's need to employ rhetoric and dialectics (see Béné, 1969, 372ff.). This final work attracted much criticism, especially since its practical advice seemed, in fact, little in tune with the actual demands of preaching. What emerges most significantly here is that it once again demonstrates how Erasmus supported his programme of Christian humanism with the authority of Augustine.

It is in the light of the above that we find the context for Erasmus's heated exchanges with Martin Luther (see Kaufman, 133ff.), emblematic of Erasmus's humanistic spirituality. Though both Reformers read Augustine, Erasmus's reading of him was responding to very different exigencies, largely determined by a methodology described as 'a theology of moderation'.[5] Unlike Luther, Erasmus totally bypassed Augustine's theological concerns for original sin and grace, believing that the basis for reform was to be found in a spiritual life nourished by Christian humanism. Moral reform would follow, as personal renewal would generate and nourish wider church reform. Thus his reading of Augustine never lost an overwhelmingly humanistic texture, the reason why the *De doctrina Christiana* remained his chief, almost sole, Augustinian text. For Luther the heart of the spiritual problems facing the church was scriptural and theological, requiring radical steps that must reach deeply into its very foundations. It was to those foundations that Luther turned his attention. Erasmus, on the other hand, firmly believed that his views were an accurate reading of Augustine, Augustine the humanist, that is. Erasmus saw that what was needed was a renewed Christian culture and it was to this task that he dedicated himself to the end of his life, 'culture at the service of piety – *une culture tout entière tournée vers la piété*' (Béné, 1986, 239).

MARTIN LUTHER (1483–1546)

When Luther received his religious habit in 1505 the Augustinian Hermits still found their claims about St Augustine being challenged. That same year Jacob Wimpfeling, a well-known Alsatian scholar, seeking to bring an end to the unedifying wrangling then plaguing theological inquiry, proposed: 'Christ is the supreme theologian to imitate and after him St Augustine above all others – *summum theologum Christum imitare et post eum divum praecipue Augustinum*' (*De Integritate* cap. 30, Schulze, 573). Irritated by the squabbling among religious orders including the Hermits and Canons, Wimpfeling wrote: 'Augustine was never a monk and never wore the cowl' (*De Integritate* 31). In 1509, in a marginal note, Luther's acerbic pen lashed out against Wimpfeling's denial of the cowl to Augustine:

> In that note we can read that Wimpfeling is a babbling driveller and ill-intentioned critic of Augustine's renown, full of envy, blind as a bat and obstinately failing to take note of the historical evidences which identify Augustine as the founder of his order. Hugh (Hugo) of St Victor quotes from Augustine's *Sermones ad Eremitas* thus confirming the foundation of the Order of Hermits by this *doctor ecclesiae*: Why, you greybeard and sickly mask, do you accuse Hugo? Why do you tell off the church of God,

> what I mean is, why with your filthy lies do you say that these sermons are not by Augustine? (WA 9,12,6–18, Schulze, 574)

At the outset of his religious life, Luther shows himself firmly committed to Augustine the monk and the authenticity of his Hermits' Augustinian way of life.

Luther's earliest formal religious and theological world was intensely Augustinian. He had entered a reformed-minded 'order within an order', a phenomenon happening throughout Catholic Europe as ancient orders found themselves confronted and challenged to renewal from within by 'observantine' breakaways, who deliberately distanced themselves from their fellow religious. They began to form new communities or took over old ones, their intention being to begin living anew in accordance with what were seen as the pristine and purer ways of an earlier more perfect age. Under the guidance of Johannes von Staupitz, the Observantine Congregation of the Augustinian Hermits to which Luther belonged looked to Augustine's *Rule* and the example of Augustine himself as inspiration for their reform. While still a young friar Luther demonstrates this clearly:

> . . . each person and above all each monk must be his own first accuser on account of his sin, and must thus live in that humility which is totally disregarded by supposedly practicing Christians. Augustine is the pattern of true monastic – and thus truly Christian – humility, because he acknowledges the rightness of God's judgment and accuses himself as a sinner without any attempt at self-justification which always ends up by putting God in the wrong. (WA 3,26,19–27,4; Schulze 575)

Through personal study, Luther came to know this Augustine even more intimately, above all the anti-Pelagian Augustine, ever dismayed by any human attempt at self-justification. But while he will eventually totally abandon the

Augustine 'of the cowl', he will remain steadfast to the anti-Pelagian Augustine.

Many issues remain under discussion regarding Luther and Augustine – the exact nature of their relationship, the quality of the impetus Luther received from within the Augustinian Hermits themselves for the reformation he was about to ignite. For our purposes, two fundamental questions need addressing. First, to what extent was Luther's theological-spiritual revolution prompted and supported by his reading of Augustine, and did that influence continue? Second, to what extent did the piety and theology of the Augustinian Hermits contribute to Luther's break with Rome? Luther himself offers us what seems to be a clear answer to the first question: 'At first I devoured Augustine; but as soon as I began to understand from Paul what justification by faith meant, I was through with him' (WATR 1,140.5–7).[6] There is no denying Luther's mature insistence that it was not Augustine but Paul who led him to his evangelical theology: it was his encounter with the word of God that taught him the true meaning and importance of faith, not anything or anyone else. The quote from Luther comes from his later writings; yet it seems clear that at critical junctures Augustine was at least 'in the wings' as Luther came to his theological breakthrough.

From 1512 on, Luther held the chair in Sacred Scripture at Wittenberg University and from his lectures there it is clear that his study of the Scriptures was aided by the study of Augustine's scriptural works. In his first lectures, on the Psalms, there is evidence that he found in Augustine supporting force for his developing sense that the church was diabolically threatened by its prosperity and complacency (Schulze, 576). Then followed lectures on Romans, Galatians and Hebrews and it is here that his 'new theology' takes clearest shape, influenced by his careful study of Augustine's *On the Spirit and the Letter* and other anti-Pelagian writings (Schulze, 577). Schulze proposes that it was this close reading of Augustine, even 'over-interpretation', that set the stage for events that were to follow:

> [T]he 'over-interpretation' is the result of the fact that in a completely new language that was free from abstract scholastic terminology Augustine introduced Luther to a Paul whom the theology of his day was willing to tolerate only with reservations. Without the anti-Pelagian Augustine there would have been no emergence of that Pauline theology in Wittenberg which was even more alien to the scholastic tradition than the theology of Augustine which in any case was already disconcerting enough. Direct access to the sources brought a new quality into the interpretation of Paul. (Schulze, 578)

It is this newly discovered Paul, reinforced by the authority of Augustine, that Luther begins to proclaim. Scholasticism must be toppled and theology must return to the Scriptures and its central affirmation: salvation is by faith alone: the justification of faith – *justificatio fidei*.

In the course of this series of disputations Luther can make the claim that Augustine is Paul's most faithful interpreter – *interpres fidelissimus* (WA I,353–74,353,14, Schulze, 579). And as Luther carried out his teaching duties at Wittenberg, he continued to assert that what he was doing was close to the heart of Augustine's own efforts: 'Our theology and St Augustine are making successful progress and prevail at our University under God's influence,' Luther could write in May of 1517 (*Correspondence* I,99, Zumkeller, 218). During this same period he found himself appointed as regional vicar of the reformed monasteries in his area. In that role we find him both criticising the principles of observance and enjoining fidelity to the Augustinian *Constitutions*.

As Luther's insistence upon justification by faith became better known, it was vociferously contested, leading to increased polemics, the accusation of heresy, and eventually threats of excommunication. That history need not be repeated here. Once Luther and Rome had irrevocably parted, did Augustine still matter for the reformer? Luther had long since reread the Fathers in the light of the doctrine of justification.

He found all wanting except Augustine: 'A *Doctor Ecclesiae* is really the product of such a controversy and such practical experience (*exercitium*) – and Augustine is almost the only one after the age of the Apostles and that of the earliest Church Fathers' (WA 30^{II},650,17–33, Schulze, 611). Yet Luther would also increasingly declare that without Pelagius it would not have been so and that if it had not been for his own immediate discovery of the doctrine of justification by faith from a personal study of the Scriptures, he would scarcely have been able to recognise even its minimal presence in the best of the Fathers. Augustine, he will insist, did *not* teach him what was most important about Christian faith: he learned that from the Scriptures; all authorities other than Scripture must be discounted: 'Let me not believe in Augustine, let us rather listen to the Scriptures – *Augustino non credam, Scripturas audiamus*' (WA 7,142,30f., Schulze, 621).[7]

Verification of this discounting of the authority of Augustine becomes even stronger when we read Luther's increasingly bitter denunciation of monasticism and eventually, its total rejection.

> What does the Rule of Augustine matter? Nowhere within it do I find faith treated. Therefore let convents (*coenobia*) either be eliminated (*eradicanda*) or reformed (*reformanda*), so that they become schools for the teaching of faith (*ut fiant scholae docendae fidei*). Very few of the ancients [he is referring to the Fathers of the Church] were concerned about faith. If Augustine had not had Pelagius, [we would find in him] nothing of faith. In Jerome we find nothing. (WA 20,775,24–776, Schulze, 579)

If Augustine the theologian is no longer Luther's teacher, Augustine the monk is ever more radically proscribed. By 1532 he will refer to the religious habit he once wore as 'the accursed cowl' (WA 30^{III},530,25f., Schulze, 585).

The previous chapter raised the question of a 'School' within the Augustinian Hermits. Students of the Protestant Reformation continue to seek to clarify the extent to which Martin

Luther's 'new theology' was the product of the influence of Augustine, the Augustinian Hermits, and Augustinian spirituality upon him. Did the Augustinian Hermits and their 'School' make possible the Protestant Reformation? Some scholars suggest a rather indirect influence, that Luther's Order was simply one part of a larger backdrop of events that set the stage for events to follow. For example, in 1506 Amerbach published his *Opera Omnia* of the works of Augustine, making possible for Luther and others a ready contact with Augustine's writings. Such publications were fostered by the humanistic return to the sources (*ad fontes*), and the Augustinian Hermits were important promoters of this renaissance. According to this analysis the Hermits would have been promoters of new critical editions and thus would have facilitated Luther's desire for a direct reading of Scripture and Augustine, but would not have predisposed him specifically to the conclusions he would reach.

Other voices, both Catholic and Protestant, have insisted on the disjunction between anything Luther may have learned as a 'Catholic theologian' and his 'new theology'. On the Catholic side, for centuries there has been a concern to highlight how Luther deviated from all that he had received while Catholic. On the Protestant side there was an equally strong concern to emphasise a total break from an irretrievably corrupt Roman church, ever sensitive to Luther's own critique: 'ungrateful papist jackasses'.[8] Recent studies suggest more subtle lines of continuity, especially the impact of Luther's mentor Staupitz and inherited theological traditions within the Augustinian Order from Gregory of Rimini and other of the Order's prominent theologians.[9] There is still little consensus and most would agree that in this regard much more work needs to be done.

Luther did indeed come out of an Augustinian reform-minded congregation that prized the study of the Bible and vigorously supported reform. Likewise, he shared with Augustine a love for the Scriptures and would agree with Augustine's oft-repeated insistence: 'Don't take my word, let us together listen to the Scriptures.' Yet in this final affirmation we find that this also is where they most differ. For Luther it was fundamentally a 'plain text', and so immediately accessible to the believer. For Augustine Scripture would always contain as much obscurity as it would lucidity, the reason why, for Augustine, it must be read 'within the church – *in ecclesia*', whereas for Luther it must be read 'within the heart – *in corde*'. Indeed, it is here, out of a difference as deep as this, that vastly different spiritualities begin to go their own way!

JOHN CALVIN (1509–1564)

There are some 1,700 explicit references to Augustine in John Calvin's writings and an additional 2,400 quotations or allusions without citation. In his most important work, *The Institutes of Christian Religion*, Augustine, after the Scriptures, is the most quoted of the Fathers, appearing some 800 times. The next closest ancient author is Gregory the Great who is cited a mere 100 times. These statistics from *The Institutes* are broadly representative of all his writings. Calvin can boldly claim: 'Augustine is so completely of our persuasion, that if I should have to make a written profession, it could be quite enough to present a composition made up entirely of excerpts from his writings.'[10] 'Augustine belongs entirely to us – *Augustinus totus noster est*' (CO 8, 266, see Van Oort, 679) is certainly the most quoted 'Augustinian' remark by Calvin.

Calvin came to Scripture and theology fresh, as it were, in the sense that he did not formally pursue a career in theology and so was not a strong supporter of a particular theological school or methodology. Thus, with a humanistic training, he could take up original texts (including Scripture) and explain them without the benefit or burden of a theological tradition that had by then become cumbersome. It is clear that early on he was predisposed to and swept into Luther's Reformation, though this is not the place to rehearse the trajectory that eventually led him to become the Genevan Reformer. What is of concern here is his place in the spiritual tradition that calls itself Augustinian.

There can be no doubt that Calvin shared with Augustine a deep concern that the biblical word be planted deep within the heart of the Christian and the Christian community. Calvin was utterly convinced that the Roman Church of his day had not only lost its scriptural authority but positively impeded faithful Christians in their access to the Bible. Augustine became for Calvin the single most important ancient authority to support this claim and provide authenticity for his campaign to restore Christianity to its authentic roots: 'It is Augustine who is the best and most faithful witness of all antiquity whom we most often cite – *quem ut optimum ex tota antiquitate et fidelissimum testem saepius citamus*' (*The Institutes*, 1559 edition, V,283–5, Van Oort, 667–8).

Yet in many ways Calvin's use of 'the Fathers', including Augustine, is primarily polemical. He was responding to challenges of innovation and deviation and he devoured Augustine in order to be able to demonstrate that the ancient church was with him – and not with his opponents. The Scriptures were all Calvin really needed – but he found himself consistently charged with departing from orthodoxy. His use of Augustine is thus very often a means to demonstrate that not he but his opponents had departed from the ancient truths. In his controversies concerning the Lord's Supper he protests: 'I advise and beseech you to charge us no longer with contradicting the ancient doctors in this case with whom we are in fact in such accord' (CO 9, 884, Van Oort, 673). Smits has collected Calvin's abundant references to the claim that 'Augustine is with us – *plane nobiscum est Augustinus*',[11] an invocation intended as much to agitate his opponents as it was to assert his unwavering conviction: 'Augustine belongs entirely to us! – *totus noster est*!' Nevertheless, Van Oort is correct in affirming that Augustine for Calvin is only a 'subsidiary authority' (698), in so far as 'Scripture alone' (*scriptura sola*) is at the heart of his understanding of reformation. It is also in this light that he can be critical of all the Fathers when he finds their expositions faulty or inadequate in holding anything not explicitly within the Scriptures. For example, he rejects the defence of prayers for the dead in Augustine's *De cura pro mortuis gerenda*[12] and critiques his predilection for allegory and his philosophising about the Scriptures. These particulars not withstanding, overall 'Calvin clearly does read his Bible with Augustinian spectacles.'[13]

This final comment is one among many which suggests that Calvin's relationship with Augustine was more than academic, that he found in him a kindred reforming spirit (for this and the following see Van Oort, 678ff.). Some but not all would even insist that Augustine played a part in Calvin's sudden conversion in 1533 or 1534 (see Marshall, 117). Calvin certainly demonstrates a careful and developed approach to reading him. For example, in his debate on freedom and grace with his Catholic opponent Albertus Pighius, he reveals not only a broad command of Augustine's works but is able to chide his opponent for taking Augustine out of context – and Calvin himself then furnishes the context.

It is in this particular controversy that he makes explicit his Augustinian hermeneutic, which he derives from Augustine's *Retractations*. He argues that the late works (i.e., anti-Pelagian) must be seen as key to the rest of Augustine's works – hence Calvin's interest in the predestination question. Van Oort has also noted that in these debates Calvin uses the humanist method, which reads original texts in context according to the intention of the author: 'Augustine must be allowed to interpret Augustine – *Augustinus suus ipse sit interpretes*.' It is on this basis that Calvin will turn again and again to Augustine, particularly in *The Institutes*, to argue the fundamental conformity between the Bishop of Hippo and Reformed theology. He has no doubts that he is the legitimate successor of Augustine's teachings and so even in his disagreements he remains respectful. Yet their relationship remained complex: when it came to the details of critical exegesis, commentators agree that Chrysostom was often Calvin's preferred choice over Augustine, the Greek Father following more consistently the sober Antiochene exegetical tradition. Further, while most assert that the notion of 'predestination', perceived by many as the cornerstone of his Reformed theology, was Calvin's greatest borrowing from Augustine, recent scholarship challenges this assertion on a variety of fronts. Some argue that Calvin misread Augustine's understanding of predestination, others insist that, in fact, predestination was not and ought not to be considered the centrepiece of Calvin's theology. The debate continues both about Augustine's and Calvin's intentions in this regard.

At the outset of *The Institutes*, John Calvin wrote: 'Nearly all the wisdom we possess, that is to say, true and sound wisdom, consists of two parts: the knowledge of God and of ourselves' (I.1). Those familiar with Augustine's *Soliloquies* will find a resonance here with Augustine's 'I desire to know God and the soul. Nothing more? Absolutely nothing' (2.1). There can be no doubt that there is much of Augustine that made its way into *The Institutes*: the centrality of Christ, the radical divine–human abyss caused by the 'original sin', the longing for the City of God (though with its distinctive Genevan realisation!), the importance of the sacraments. Smits can thus conclude that Calvin's thought has an Augustinian and evangelical character: 'He was convinced of the fundamental accord between his own teaching and Augustine's' (Smits, 265). Yet it has also been repeatedly emphasised by Calvin scholars that what remained foundational for Calvin was 'justification by faith' – and in that sense he remained ever the Protestant Reformer, kindred spirit (despite their differences) with Martin Luther. Smits sums up well the nature of the relationship:

> Calvin shows a real preoccupation to cover himself with the authority of Augustine in the questions of predestination, sacraments, and original sin. His reasons for this are, first, the veneration which his adversaries, be they Catholic or Protestant, felt for the bishop of Hippo, and then the fact that he himself had discovered in Augustine's

> writings the fundamental principle of the Reformation, namely, *the radical corruption of the human heart* [italics mine].[14]

The piety associated with Calvin has often been caricatured as both gloomy and rigorous, emphasising the human–divine abyss, with subsequent centuries taking this one step further and identifying it with the Augustine discovered by Calvin. But if it is true that the foundational principle of the Reformation was 'the radical corruption of the human heart', it is clear that Augustine's spiritual vision and intentions were elsewhere. Placing Christ at the centre of the human heart was his singular intent. Thus, it may be the case that the very acrimony surrounding the controversies of the Reformation prevented a more comprehensive and integral assessment of what was truly at the centre of Augustine's spiritual vision.

JEROME SERIPANDO (1493–1563)

The final 'Augustinian portrait' to be considered in this century of reformation is of a figure too little known outside the circle of those who are familiar with the Council of Trent (1545–63) and the Counter-Reformation, the Roman Catholic response not only to the Protestant Reformation but also to a long-standing call from within Roman Catholicism itself to address the issue of reform. Jerome Seripando emerged as a leading Catholic and explicitly Augustinian voice in the early stages of Trent's reforms. In his day he enjoyed an eminent reputation: scholar and theologian, friar and religious superior, Prior General of the Augustinians, Cardinal and Papal Legate at the Council of Trent, and, at time of his death, Archbishop of Salerno. Sincerely religious, brilliant and well educated, ardent reformer, experienced church leader, he represents an Augustinian voice working within the institutional framework of Roman Catholicism as it struggled to face the spiritual crisis generated by this century of reform. A renewed interest today in the figure of Seripando is part of a wider revival of studies concerning the Tridentine reform. Seripando's efforts are important for our study here since they unfold within a clearly Augustinian context.

Seripando was born into a noble Neapolitan family, prominent members of a social class that had contributed their sons to the service of both church and monarchy.[15] Orphaned shortly after birth, he was reared by an uncle who saw to his receiving an excellent liberal education. Because Naples was participating in the humanistic revolution sweeping Italy, Seripando was able to avail himself of the finest instructors in Greek, Latin, Hebrew, literature and philosophy, and all the other components of a humanist education. It is suggested that his predilection for humanistic studies led to his decision to enter the Augustinian Order, taking the habit of a novice in 1507. Among their membership were leading voices in the Italian humanist movement, and they were known for their circle at Santo Spirito in Florence, one frequented by prominent figures such as Boccaccio and Petrarch.

Within the Augustinian Hermits his talents were immediately recognised, and he was sent to the Order's best houses of study. After ordination in 1512 he was called to Rome and assigned the task of keeping the confidential register of the Prior General, the official record of the Order's acts and decrees. During this period he also began to gain renown as a preacher, even delivering sermons before the Emperor, Charles V. In 1523 he was made Vicar General of his Augustinian Congregation in Naples, an observantine 'order within an order'. In this capacity he aggressively carried out a programme of reform and renewal. During a time when religious leadership was more often than not noted for its absenteeism, Seripando visited each community of his reform Congregation within the Augustinian Hermits, spoke to each individual member, and delivered noteworthy sermons imbued with Augustinianism, humanism and Christian Platonism. With the election of Paul III in 1534 Seripando found himself called to Rome by the Pope to preach. While there he enjoyed the Pope's confidence. As his preaching tasks spread throughout

Italy, he became increasingly informed not only of the spiritual condition of the church in Italy but also about the theology and spirituality of the Protestant Reformers, having had since 1531 permission to study their writings.[16] While he makes no explicit mention of this study in his preaching, commentators note that he often spoke of 'justification of the sinner by faith and love, through the merits of Jesus Christ'.[17] In 1539 he was elected Prior General of the Augustinian Order (his name being proposed to the Augustinians by Paul III) and now his attention to the question of reform was to take two separate but related directions. Negatively he sought to purge the Order of any Lutheran tendencies; positively he sought to reinvigorate the spiritual and theological life of the community.

Regarding efforts at purging the Order of any latent Protestantism, Seripando reflects the temper of the times. Thus he passed decrees providing for imprisonment and even condemnation to the galleys for those convicted of 'Lutheranism' (see Cesareo, 27). Yet these harsh measures were far overshadowed by his positive calls for both institutional and personal renewal within the Order. For Seripando this meant a return to living the communal life, according to the spirit and letter of the Augustinian *Rule*. He was equally concerned with the reinvigoration of the intellectual life of the Order. To accomplish this reform he undertook a lengthy and demanding personal visitation of the houses of the Order in Italy, France, Spain and Portugal. The culmination of all these efforts took the form of a renewal of the *Constitutions* of the Augustinian Hermits, with legislation that called for greater emphasis on studies, a uniform teaching by its professors, and an insistence that the illustrious doctors of the Order, beginning with Giles of Rome, be followed. One commentator sees in this a clear indication of a sense of a distinctive 'Augustinian school',[18] but for our purposes what is more important is that it evidences a spirituality grounded in theology and imbued with a deep love for the tradition of the church. Seripando's 'Augustinianism' is thoroughly 'Catholic' in its framework:

> Professors of the Bible, in their interpretation of sacred letters, must not audaciously dissent from the teachings of the holy doctors of the Church nor teach anything that is not in accordance with the decrees of the Holy Roman Church and of the sacred Councils approved by her. (*Constitutiones OESA*, Rome, 1551, cap. 37)

Both humility and a forceful ecclesial framework stand out in this excerpt from Seripando's *Constitutions.*

Certainly for those most interested in the Catholic reforming efforts of the Council of Trent, the name of Seripando is of critical importance. His labours in this regard demonstrate a deeply Augustinian spirit. He first participated as Prior General of the Augustinians, lending his mind and voice to its earliest sessions. He fought vigorously for the right of religious orders to continue preaching and not be subject to local bishops. He fought even more vigorously for bishops to maintain active residence in and personal governance of their dioceses, arguing so far as to propose 'residency as divine law (*ius divinum*)' (Cesareo, 34). He likewise actively took part in the debates about original sin and justification, offering what he considered to be an Augustinian position on these questions. Here we see him highlighting once again the importance of faith and baptism, emphasising a central Augustinian insistence 'that all depends upon God' (Cesareo, 33). In 1551 Seripando made it clear that he would not accept another term as Prior General, a bout of poor health nourishing his certainty that death was near. His retirement, which unfortunately was persistently interrupted, included an episcopal nomination which he succeeded in turning down for reasons of health. By 1553, however, his health had returned and he found himself unable to refuse a nomination as Archbishop of Salerno, Italy. There he implemented an ambitious programme for reform, taking Augustine as his model and guide. Residency and personal governance were its presuppositions, as well as an energetic programme of preaching, visitation and legislative reforms. His sermons manifest a familiarity with Augustine's preaching and actualize the Bishop of Hippo's own practice.

> . . . the Christian life ought not and cannot be only contemplative or only active. Rather it is necessary for it to be mixed (*utrumque misceri*). A Christian needs not only a love of truth which leads to contemplation but the affection of charity, the well-spring of action. The Christian life is thus based on these two factors. How can a true Christian so give himself to contemplation so as not to leave it for action when he hears his neighbour's need for the service of love? This was Augustine's advice to monks: 'If the Church requires your ministry, don't accept it out of prideful greed nor reject it out of laziness. Rather, obey God with a tranquil heart.' (Augustine, *ep.* 48.2)[19]

In the meantime he was appointed to the Roman Inquisition where he sought to have charity rather than castigation serve as principal means for winning back those who had gone astray (Cesareo, 39). Did Seripando learn this from his Augustinian *Rule*, with its emphasis on healing sinners and not simply punishing them? In 1561 Pius IV recognised his talents once again by elevating him to the Cardinalate and appointing him a Papal Legate to the Council. Thus he became a member of a supervisory committee of five which had responsibility for the Council's labours. He participated energetically in the preparatory drafting of decrees to be discussed as well as in the actual discussion. Once again, his interventions centre on matters he considered essential for the renewal of the church: the question of episcopal residency, decrees concerning the sacraments and Mass, and most especially the Council's debates on justification.

Regarding justification, his position was argued from Augustinian texts. It is in these discussions that we see the culmination of Seripando's Augustinian efforts. What emerges is a forthright evangelical insistence upon a thoroughly Augustinian interpretation of justification by faith.[20] Such an emphasis even prompted whisperings of a crypto-Lutheranism in his position. Surely it was his very own reading of Augustine, influenced by the affectivity of the then current spirituality, that led to his emphasis in these discussions on the *experience* of faith in baptism. 'Baptism does not cleanse except through faith' was Seripando's proposal for the decree on original sin and justification; the Council, instead, insisted on the centrality of the rite, with its final formulation emphasising 'through the sacrament of baptism, conferred according to the ritual of the church'.[21] Likewise, he proposed that the Council consider the question of a 'double justification – *duplex iustificatio*', the notion that a 'first' justification through faith, leads to a 'second', manifest in hope and love. Once again he found himself representing a minority view. In this he did indeed take ideas from Augustine, but offered them according to the categories and terminology of Scholastic theology. What is also of interest was his attempt to build a bridge between what he recognised as authentic insights of the Reformers and the church's need for reform; he insisted in good Augustinian fashion (*conf.* 12.25.34): 'Whoever speaks something true, even if a heretic, is speaking that truth from the Holy Spirit.'[22]

One last dimension of Seripando's Augustinianism deserves mention. One of the most important documents he left behind was a diary, a personal journal where he recorded and commented upon the events he lived and witnessed, from the sadness and pain of a divided church, to earthquake, plague, Turkish invasion, and even to dental problems (as Augustine also does in *conf.* 9.4.12). His times were not kind. He comments on his diary to a friend, and in so doing, suggests that they were becoming his own *Confessions*:

> I am a student of God's book of providence, the providence God has in his infinite goodness deigned to show me throughout the course of my life, which I can indeed call: *in laboribus a iuventute mea* [in labours from my youth]. You cannot imagine how much I see clearly and how much I touch with my own hands in a certain *ephemeride* (diary),

> how I have written principally concerning the things which have happened to me in this life, God's providence on my behalf: something noted by me so often, but never as much as in the present.[23]

In many ways it seemed that events overtook Seripando. He could not hold back the dissolution of many German Augustinian monasteries as they succumbed to reforming voices other than his own. Many of his specific interventions went unheeded at the Council of Trent, his theological insights even troubling some. Yet, there can be no doubt that his efforts at reform within the Order paved the way for a new flowering of the Augustinian Order, above all in Italy and Spain.[24] Likewise, his time as Archbishop of Salerno set a model for the kind of episcopacy necessary in the post-Tridentine reform he did so much to foster. Indeed Seripando not only felt himself a member of the 'community of Augustine' but equally a student in the 'school of Augustine', doing his utmost to realise in himself the ideals modelled by Augustine, as evidenced in his preaching:

> Augustine wants bishops to not only teach with prudence, but also to learn with patience. It is, in fact, necessary that the bishop not only teach, but also learn. That one is the best teacher who daily grows and makes progress by learning even better things. (*Discorsi* 109–11)

Seripando sought to embody the spirituality of Augustine and found himself placed in roles of leadership and responsibility within his Order and on behalf of the church at large where that spirituality could serve as a catalyst for solid reform and renewal.

CONCLUSION

Erasmus, Luther, Calvin and Seripando: taken together they mirror the complex richness and conflicting reception of the Augustinian tradition in this century of reform. Erasmus found in Augustine the foundations of a Christian humanism, generating a piety sceptical of theological wrangling. Luther found there a lonely ancient voice proclaiming justification by faith (*justificatio fidei*). Calvin found in Augustine a kindred spirit, a God-centredness that relativised all else. Seripando found in Augustine a model bishop and man of the church who offered example and teaching for true reform. Of the four, Seripando most openly and unapologetically identified his own entire journey with that of Augustine. As monk, theologian and bishop he clearly sought to lay claim to the whole of Augustine's own spiritual vision. In the centuries to follow such a claim will become increasingly difficult to make. If at the beginning of the sixteenth century the voice of Augustine was universally recognised in the Christian West as the pre-eminent spiritual and theological authority, the century ends with clashing and competing Augustinian voices. Augustinianism, in the centuries that follow, will more often than not be a debate about which of these voices is truly that of Augustine.

6. PILGRIMS TO THE SELF: MODERN AND POSTMODERN AUGUSTINIANS

In the aftermath of the contentious sixteenth century, readings of Augustine in the modern period will more often than not bear the marks of that century's ruptures and controversies. 'Modern' here is obviously a relative term, referring to Augustine's place in a world marked not only by a divided Christian Europe, but also by an emerging science and technology, often proposing its truth claims as an alternative to Christianity. This challenge will not be without enormous spiritual consequences. With foundations shaken by religious change and sectarian warfare, a variety of thinkers turned away from religion altogether, in search of more secure and less contested spiritual sanctuary grounded in the human self or conceptions of a pristine natural order without God. Such non-religious methods were often met by doctrinal rigidity or anti-theological spiritual retreat, only further problematising a perceived divide between the human and the divine. As will become evident in what follows, both Cartesianism and Jansenism can be seen as manifestations of such tensions. Each of these positions came to be associated with Augustine and each in its own way lent a helping hand to the construction of the modern self, often a shipwrecked self, proclaiming either a radical autonomy before God or a radical alienation from God. Tragically, the skewed and partial readings of Augustine that resulted, each with its own particular form of spiritual pessimism, are even today all too uncritically labelled 'Augustinian'.

A striking element of this modern period will be readings of Augustine where the 'theological' Augustine gives way entirely to the 'philosophical' Augustine. What may be described as a 'spirituality of the self', linked to Augustine and drawing heavily upon his texts, laden with an acute concern for 'the subject' and ostensibly aggressively a-theological, will be its product. An intriguing example of this is to be found in the postmodernist philosopher Jacques Derrida. This final chapter's excursion into the history of the Augustinian spiritual tradition, spanning over four centuries down to the present day, will be able to offer only a cursory survey of some key moments in modern as well as contemporary spiritual seeking where Augustine's role was or is prominent. Underlying each brief excursion are enormous debates that continue to this day. I begin with the movement called Jansenism, turn then to Descartes and his revolution, move on to readings of Augustine by the philosophers Blondel and Derrida, and conclude with a brief excursion into contemporary Augustinian developments. Indeed, throughout the modern period, Augustine's spiritual journey will continue to invite and provoke engagement.

A TYRANNY OF GRACE: THE JANSENIST CONTROVERSY[1]

Cornelis Janssen (1585–1638) was known to have read the complete works of Augustine ten times and his anti-Pelagian writings thirty times. In the funeral oration spoken at his obsequies the Premonstratentian J. ven den Steen quoted Jansenius, his more familiar name in history, to the effect that while the 'other Fathers are useful, Augustine [alone] is necessary'.[2] His eulogist spoke warmly of Jansenius' holiness and piety as well as the depth of his theological learning, noting that he kept Augustine ever present in his theological labours and read him as a son, a novice and a disciple, but never as a '*doctor*' (i.e., he always read him to learn) (Orcibal, 308).

The label 'Jansenist' would be welcomed by few today as complimentary. It implies that one is rigid, rigorist, puritanical. Jansenius is most famous for his massive tome titled *Augustinus*, described by one of the most qualified scholars on the topic as arguably the 'least read yet most attacked' book ever written.[3] Jansenius wrote his *Augustinus* both to accuse and to refute the perceived Pelagians of his day. Associated with his name and its controversies are the 'French School' and Cardinal Berulle, the Founder of the Oratorians, as well as the Parisian monastery of Port-Royal, and the names of Saint-Cyran, Arnaud and Pascal.[4] Likewise linked to the name Jansenism were bitter battles between theological positions such as Baianism, Molinism and Quietism. And underlying these erudite disputes were practical questions concerning Christian piety and virtuous living, with writers such as Fénelon, Bossuet and Madame Guyon producing spiritual best-sellers for a devoted readership.

The Jansenist Controversy marks a time after Trent when concerns for orthodoxy within Catholicism ran high. Threats of Index or Inquisition were everyday facts of life for ecclesiastics of all stripes, and charges and countercharges of laxism or rigorism were the order of the day. Public theological polemics were commonplace and even led to the suppression of the Jesuits in 1771 by Pope Clement XIV. A 'theatre of war' is how one scholar describes the charged atmosphere surrounding the Jansenist Controversy.[5] Recent studies, seeking to reconstruct original intentions and contexts, have called into question some traditional perceptions regarding this complex period in the history of Christian spirituality.[6] What is most important here is the explicit link that Jansenius sought to create between himself and his chosen spiritual father Augustine, and the impact that this 'Jansenist Augustine' has had on subsequent developments, perceptions and receptions of the Augustinian spiritual tradition.

What did Jansenius intend? What did he teach? In what sense was it 'Augustinian'? Answers to these questions have deep implications for Augustinian spirituality if, in fact, Jansenius' reading of Augustine was accurate. For Jansenius the heart of the question he pursued in his *Augustinus* was indeed close to Augustine's heart: grace and free will. But it was in the light of very specific contemporary (late-sixteenth-century and beyond) controversies regarding grace and free will that

Jansenius turned to Augustine. During his earliest days of theological study he came to the resolve to return theology to its primitive purity and purge it of philosophical (Aristotelian-Scholastic) contamination (Ceyssens, 1982, 14). And early on he discovered this purity in Augustine; the more he read him, the more he was convinced that the subsequent tradition, certainly the theologians of his day, had distorted the teaching of the Doctor of Grace. Yet while he was absorbing Augustine's theology of grace, it was always in the light of his seventeenth-century theological context, with its distinctive methods, its peculiar vocabulary and its precise concerns. In fact, the grace controversies seething at the time had created such a climate of tension that Pope Clement VIII felt compelled to call together a special commission (the *Congregationes de auxiliis*) to put an end to the theological quarrelling. He encouraged all to turn to Augustine, the Doctor of Grace, to put an end to the rancour – 'know the mind of Augustine – *scire mentem Augustini*' was the Pope's remedy (Ceyssens, 1982, 17).

This is exactly what Jansenius set out to do: offer a comprehensive historical and synthetic analysis of grace, based upon the teaching of Augustine. He completed the work shortly before succumbing to the plague in 1638, and despite its ravages, he died in peace, content that his life's work was accomplished. It is important to note that he viewed the work as an historical study, not a treatise of speculative theology. He expected his critics to judge whether or not he had read Augustine correctly and not to criticise it as an exercise in theological thinking. He was not proposing himself but Augustine. If he had read him correctly, and the theology was wrong, then the church would have to condemn Augustine.

What has been labelled the Jansenist Controversy erupted two years after his death, upon the posthumous printing of *Augustinus* in 1640. The year coincided with the centenary of the approbation of the Jesuits – and it would be members of the Society of Jesus who would be Jansenius' most vocal critics (Ceyssens, 1982, 23). *Augustinus* was written in a polished Latin and comprised three heavy volumes; the first dealt with an historical analysis of Pelagianism; the second discussed creation, the fall, and the concept of 'pure nature' (is it possible to consider real human happiness and fulfilment apart from God? No, said Jansenius); the third volume dealt with the nature of grace, its operation and results. It was his notion of 'victorious delight (*delectatio victrix*)' – God infallibly attracts us to good by means of delight – in the final volume that generated the most debate. In the last analysis he was read as proposing that there is no human effort involved in the pursuit of holiness – and that this was the teaching of Augustine.

Did Jansenius read Augustine correctly? For example, he was intensely concerned to deny any purely 'natural' end for humanity and could find support in Augustine's 'you have made us for yourself, O Lord' of the opening lines of the *Confessions*. Overall, however, he rigidly systematised Augustine's teaching on grace and free will and read him through a grid overlaid with centuries of synthesis and precision unknown to Augustine. Jansenius tried to elaborate in detail what Augustine preferred to affirm on the level of spiritual and theological principle and mystery: God's sovereignty. Further, many commentators suggest that Jansenius' approach to grace bypassed the 'ontological' and focused on the 'psychological' – that is, he turned to the experiential and volitional, with insufficient attention to foundational questions regarding divine and human natures as well as divine agency and human freedom.

It is also clear that Jansenius the theologian should be distinguished from Jansenism the movement. Cornelius Jansen, Bishop of Ypres, intended to write a work in historical theology. Jansenism as a movement nurtured an intransigent and pessimistic form of Catholicism, still spontaneously linked by many to Augustine. Ultimately, Jansenius' exercise in positive theology, his *Augustinus*, was in fact a very partial reading of Augustine, further complicated by its overly rigid and highly systematised resolution of a host of issues surrounding questions of grace and free will, sin and human nature that Augustine indeed proposed but never claimed to solve.

Where Augustine sought conversion and humility before the mystery of grace, Jansenius sought precision.[7] It was to problematise many subsequent efforts to read Augustine.

MY MIND AND I: CARTESIAN INTERIORITY AND THE MODERN SELF

'*Cogito, ergo sum*': surely no single philosophical statement is better known than René Descartes's (1596–1650) famous dictum from his *Meditations*: 'I think, therefore I am.' Antoine Arnauld, 'the intellectual leader of the Jansenist movement',[8] an avowed 'Augustinian' and one of Descartes's correspondents, was much taken by the philosopher's work. Having read the *Meditations* he wrote to Descartes, with these comments:

> Here it first occurs [to me] to marvel, that the most eminent man [Descartes] has established as the first principle of his philosophy the same thing that was established by the divine Augustine, a man of the most acute intellect and entirely admirable, not only in theological but also in philosophical matters. (Arnauld, *Fourth Set of Objections*, Menn, 4)

Arnaud saw a direct link between Descartes's '*cogito ergo sum*' and Augustine. He went on to point out a specific passage from the *De Libero Arbitrio* (2.3.7) where Augustine develops his own argument for existence based upon the evidence of the self.

Another correspondent, Père Mersenne, close friend of Descartes and dedicated mathematician, noted an even more striking similarity between Descartes's '*cogito*' and a passage from the *City of God* (11.26). Here, in addressing ancient sceptics, Augustine used the argument, 'if I err, I am – *si enim fallor, sum*.'

> For if I err (*fallor*), I am (*sum*). Indeed someone who is not (*non est*), is not able to err (*falli*); thus by this very

> reason, I am (*sum*), if I err (*fallor*). Therefore I am (*ergo sum*), if I err (*fallor*); for how is it possible to err (*fallor*), when I am certain to exist (*esse*) if I err (*fallor*)? (*civ.* 11.26)

The 'certainty' of erring thus becomes an affirmation of existence and contradicts the very 'uncertainty' of existence the sceptics posit. Mersenne saw a close affinity between Descartes's '*cogito ergo sum*' and Augustine's '*fallor ergo sum*', but his suggestion of the Augustinian character of Descartes's argument did not end there. He began a virtual 'Augustinian' campaign on Descartes's behalf: 'the more learned someone becomes in the teaching of Augustine,' he insisted, 'the more willingly he will embrace Cartesian philosophy' (Menn, 17). If Mersenne had no doubts regarding his 'Augustinianness', Descartes himself was not so inclined. In fact, he resisted all efforts to attribute his foundational insight to the Bishop of Hippo. He replies to still another correspondent, Colvius, in this vein:

> I am obliged to you for drawing my attention to the passage of St Augustine relevant to my [*I think, therefore I am*]. I went today to the library of this town to read it, and I found that he does really use it to prove the certainty of our existence. He goes on to show that there is a certain likeness of the Trinity in us, in that we exist, we know that we exist, and we love the existence and the knowledge we have. I, on the other hand, use the argument to show that this 'I' which is thinking is an immaterial substance with no bodily element. These are two very different things. In itself it is such a simple and natural thing to infer that one exists from the fact that one is doubting that it could have occurred to any writer. But I am glad to find myself in agreement with St Augustine, if only to hush the little minds who have tried to find fault with the principle. (Descartes to Colvius, 14 November 1640)[9]

Descartes does two noteworthy things here. He minimises the importance of Augustine's insight; yet he does appreciate the 'coincidence' of their ideas as a way of silencing the many critics of his 'new philosophy'.

These conversations between Descartes and his circle only helped to fuel much subsequent discussion regarding the precise nature of Descartes's relationship to Augustine, certainly an important question for the history of philosophy but, in the case of this study, vitally significant for the modern reception of the Augustinian tradition. The 'self' that emerges from the Cartesian debates has often been identified as 'the modern self', and its make-up has profound implications for modern spirituality. Did Descartes learn of that self from Augustine? Descartes himself insists that he did not. Subsequent commentators are divided. Some say: if the foundation and authority of his '*cogito*' is the thinking subject itself, an irreparable breach would have been created in his argument by suggesting that he discovered this principle elsewhere than in the 'thinking self', Descartes's thinking self, of course. They add that after his death, Cartesian supporters, both enthralled with his method and concerned with challenges to his orthodoxy, undertook an aggressive campaign to show how Descartes's thought coincided with that of the 'great Bishop of Hippo'. Descartes could thus emerge as good Catholic thinker.

There is little doubt of their affinity at certain levels. Augustine's constant call to rise above the senses, especially when the question is one of true wisdom, strikes a resonant chord with Descartes's attempt to ground knowledge beyond bodily perception. Accordingly, his 'carving out' of a great interiority where he can locate a secure knowledge can be certainly perceived to have an Augustinian ring to it. Likewise Descartes's explicit anti-Scholastic and anti-Aristotelian approach to truth finds a more kindred home in Augustine's Platonism and its pre-Scholastic method of interiority. Undoubtedly regarding the role of God in Descartes's philosophy, much can be seen to be in common with Augustine, above all God's role as a guarantor of knowledge – though debate still rages over the nature of the God of Cartesian certitude (see Matthews, 169ff., Menn, 262ff.).

Most importantly, Augustine's intention was never solely philosophical but Descartes's plainly was. Augustine's consideration of interiority and self was always an integral dimension of a deliberate theological and spiritual project: conversion, humility, seeking the face of God (contemplation). Descartes's project, on the other hand, was primarily epistemological and metaphysical (cognition). He wanted to construct a 'new philosophy' whose certainty stood over and against a Scholasticism seen as bankrupt. Descartes's philosophy was meant to stand solitary and secure upon the groundwork of the certainty of the rational self. Augustine's interior self is anchored in biblical faith, where reason is complementary to the kind of faith implied by the biblical text: 'unless you believe, you will not understand' (Isaiah 7:9, LXX). Descartes's 'rational project', his effort to establish a certitude apart from the senses, demanded a sharp distinction between mind and body and traversed a path very different from Augustine's 'spiritual project'. Rather than a concern about mind/body separation, Augustine was seeking salvation for mind *and* body. This is not meant to dismiss Descartes's intention; it simply notes the difference of intention and perspective.

Descartes's strict insistence on the mind/body split has also led some thinkers to align him with Augustine, each one said to represent a long philosophical/spiritual tradition of dualism. Yet, while Descartes's intention in the 'split' was certainty, i.e., certain knowledge, Augustine's concern was with a certainty of a different order, i.e., with saving knowledge. In dealing with body/mind questions, Augustine's interest is above all theological/ascetical, and he consistently sees greater danger in 'mind deception' than 'sense deception' – the angels fell not because of 'sense deception' but because of pride – as did Adam and Eve. It is enough to read Augustine's abundant discussions of the soul's relationship to the body in order to discover that, while there are deep underlying philosophical positions involved, his concerns remain primarily religious; for example, how is original sin passed on in such a way that it affects not just the body but equally the soul? Further, it is clear that there was much development in his thinking in this regard, stimulated both by a maturing resurrection theology as well as anti-Pelagian debates concerning nature and original sin and similar questions that required deeper inquiry into the nature of the body/soul relationship.[10]

Yet what is the import of such arguments in a book on a spiritual tradition, in a consideration of Augustinian spirituality? The question is critical precisely because of its implications regarding the 'modern self'. If one could speak of some strands of modern spirituality as exhibiting the Cartesian split (mind/body, interior/exterior, objective/subjective, etc.) and/or privileging 'subjectivity', and if in some way this can be traced back to Augustine, the importance of the question for the Augustinian tradition becomes clear.[11] Gohier has concluded that there is surface resemblance but foundational dissimilarity between the two thinkers.[12] Menn proposes a deep, if not always obvious, coherence. He provocatively argues that the interior discipline laid out by Descartes has much in common with Augustine, so that the two share a contemplative approach to truth, a way of 'conceiving the soul and God' (Menn, 394) that takes place *within*, this intellectual intuition grounding an ascent to truth. In that sense, according to Menn, the subsequent tradition identified with Descartes, Cartesianism, was not true to Descartes – nor to Augustine.

Cartesianism, whatever its actual relationship to Descartes, fostered an autonomous and dichotomised self that would be most inhospitable to an Augustinian self, one aware of inner conflict, yearning for the certitude and peace of communion and wholeness, and knowing that such profound peace and satisfaction can only be found in God. The lonely Cartesian self stands in stark clinical contrast with the Augustinian self of restless heart narrated in his *Confessions*, where ultimate certitude is no less than the love of God.

RESTLESS SEEKERS: AUGUSTINE AND THE PHILOSOPHERS

The Cartesian-Augustine question is one instance of a broader modern philosophical interest in Augustine that has attracted thinkers representing a wide range of positions. From Kierkegaard to Wittgenstein, Husserl to Heidegger, Camus to Hannah Arendt, Max Scheler to Karl Jaspers, many modern philosophers have found Augustine to be a provocative if not always kindred partner for dialogue. It suggests what has been repeated a number of times throughout this study, that in the Augustinian tradition critical inquiry can be considered a spiritual practice: disciplined and thoughtful spiritual searching has an important role to play in Augustinian spirituality.

It is clear that the questions, content and method of Augustine's writings have attracted philosophers of differing if not mutually exclusive perspectives. Some of these philosophical encounters have completely bypassed or even sought to undermine the God-centredness of Augustine that permeates every aspect of his thought, while others have identified with his thought in such a way that their philosophical project takes on an intensely spiritual, even mystical dimension. One way to demonstrate this diversity is to look at two radically contrasting philosophical approaches to Augustine. In unique and provocative ways both are spiritually oriented, both come out of a French philosophical tradition, both are marked by an effort to redirect philosophical discourse. When viewed together they exemplify the divergence which readings of Augustine can prompt. The first philosopher to be considered, Maurice Blondel, was a thoroughly Catholic thinker, avowedly committed to a revitalisation of 'Catholic' philosophy, and one who saw in such a project a source for deep spiritual renewal. The second is the postmodernist Jacques Derrida, representing an approach to philosophy which is broadly speaking iconoclastic, intensely wary of metaphysical claims, intent upon singularity, coping with a deconstructed self.

Blondel (1861–1949) is a rich and compelling figure who represents well the ferment in French philosophical thought and especially Catholic thought that marked the last decades of the nineteenth and the first half of the twentieth century. His first published work *Action: Essay on a Critique of Life and a Science of Practice* (1893) proposed an existential approach to philosophy, which contrasted sharply with the then prevailing direction of nineteenth-century French Catholic Thomism. He speaks (in the third person) of his intention:

> 'Yes or no, does life have a meaning and does man [*sic*] have a destiny?' It is the essential human question and, as such, the essential philosophical question. The author wants to show that our acts themselves imply the solution. We cannot avoid acting, and every attempt to limit the scope and interpretation of our actions will push us beyond itself until finally we are faced with the question of the supernatural, a question that we can neither properly pose nor answer without going beyond our own resources.[13]

The work generated much reaction and a number of thinkers were struck by what they perceived as Blondel's Augustinian rather than Thomistic approach to philosophy. At the time, however, Blondel had only a superficial acquaintance with Augustine and the controversy surrounding his own work provoked in him a serious turn to Augustine's writings. All the while engaged in the task of showing the complementariness of Aquinas and Augustine, his thinking nonetheless began to take on a markedly Augustinian dynamism, with a thrust towards the existential and a concern for the operation of the will. He consolidated a lifetime of effort in this regard in an essay on Augustine written in 1930 on the occasion of the fifteenth centenary of Augustine's death: 'The Latent Resources in Augustine's Thought'.[14]

By the time of its writing Blondel was virtually blind and so could not turn to his own beloved books and notes. This handicap left its mark on the essay as, relying on memory and insight, he intuitively summed up his decades-long absorption with Augustine. He proposed both a method to read Augustine and a unifying centre for Augustine's thought: 'Every one of his statements . . . implies the whole body of his doctrine' (Blondel, 322). To read Augustine according to his own intention, Blondel insists, requires that he must be read integrally. He laments those self-styled disciples of Augustine who in claiming allegiance to him have done a great disservice by their partial readings, 'separating' the great antitheses within his thought: knowledge/wisdom, dialectics/illumination, reason/faith, exterior/interior, particular/universal, experience/intuition, inner life/human history. They are meant to be kept together in dynamic contrast.

> . . . in the philosophy of the saint we find in an implicit, but yet most live, form, a synthesis, or rather, a vital unity which allows each of these elements its legitimate share: hereditary fatalities, conscious experiences, rational elaboration, triumph of the spirit life, conflicts of the will, the influence of grace; all in admirable harmony in the stupendous tilting ground which is the soul, and in which all nature, the human will, and divine assistance compete together for the prize. (Blondel, 333–4)

It is for this reason that he calls Augustine's philosophy an 'integral philosophy', one whose horizon is wide enough to encompass both God and humanity. This is precisely where he sees the 'centre', the 'profound unity without which it is impossible to grasp his real thought'.

> Man [*sic*] is not a light unto himself; nothing that we know is luminous. To seek for light, to tend towards truth, is not to get to know things, objects, facts of consciousness, rational ideas, transcendentals; all that, which we imagine to be the first step in the ascent to God, gives us no enlightenment; it is what needs to be enlightened, because it has no truth except that which comes from God . . . '*ubi inveni veritatatem, inveni Deum.*' (Blondel, 337–8)

The final words are from the *Confessions*: 'Wherever I find truth, there I find God.'[15] Blondel goes on:

> If we think that we can be at home within ourselves, it is because we have failed to get to know our very own being. God is more intimate to us that our own intimacy. Of God I must say: '*intus est, ego foris*' [see *conf.* 7.7.11; also 10.27.38]. Whether I climb to the summit of myself or sink to the lowest depth, I find only a void in what is peculiarly myself, and that void was made, and can only be filled, for and by God. (Blondel, 338)

The Blondelian self, in deep resonance with Augustine, is indeed a 'self-in-God'. He reads Augustine as insisting that humanity is ordained for God's own life and that it is here that one finds the centre of his thought, though not in a way that confuses the divine with the human, or allows the one to simply absorb the other. And this truth is discovered not by 'knowing' truth but by 'encountering' it, reflecting the personalism Blondel found in Augustine: God is a *who*, not a *what*. Much more could be said here of Blondel's reading of Augustine but what is perhaps most important to note is his attempt to engage Augustine on his own terms, to look at him integrally, and embrace the divine–human intimacy that holds Augustine's thought together. Blondel's spiritual importance in the history of Augustinianism lies precisely here. His writings convey both the intimacy of faith and the rigour of thinking that were characteristic of the Bishop of Hippo himself.

Yet for all his love of Augustine he maintained critical distance: he laments his 'ambiguity' on certain questions – freedom, for example, since it made his thought vulnerable to mistaken readings; he acknowledged that he could be out of date and even wrong on some points. Yet, in the last analysis, Blondel saw Augustine as offering the best hope for a 'Catholic philosophy', one that is both authentically spiritual and intellectually respectable:

> The Augustinian outlook alone allows not only the Cath-

> olic philosophy, but also the fully human one. If this has not yet been fully realized, the reason is that the future reserves for the doctrine of St Augustine a fruitful activity far surpassing all the influence it has exercised in the past. (Blondel, 353)

Blondel learned from Augustine that engagement with God need not abandon thoughtfulness nor a concern for the human. Faith and reason, action and intuition can work together to find truth in God; philosophy is meant to be a spiritual practice.

Postmodernism is a charged and often contentious term that has made its presence felt in many disciplines, including religion and philosophy. While in general it may be said to be a critique of the certainty and absolutes of modern thought, of its nature it is difficult to define, the widely diverse movement resisting the very notion of the fixed and the final that any definition seems to imply. Its approaches are often described as idiosyncratic and this perhaps well describes the conversations of postmodernists with Augustine. One suggestive though brief look at the resulting encounter, in this case how the French thinker Jacques Derrida (1930–) reads Augustine, will make this clear.[16] It will also provide an interesting contrast with the approach of Blondel.

Derrida speaks of his peculiar bond with the Bishop of Hippo:

> The way I refer to St Augustine is really not very orthodox; it is rather – a sin! I have to confess that my relation to St Augustine's *Confessions* is a little strange. If I had to summarize what I am doing with St Augustine in *Circumfession*, I would say this. On the one hand, I play with some analogies, that he came from Algeria, that his mother died in Europe, the way my mother was dying when I was writing this, and so on. I am constantly playing, seriously playing, with this, and quoting sentences from the *Confessions* in Latin, all the while trying, through my love and admiration for St Augustine – I

> have enormous and immense admiration for him – to ask questions about a number of axioms, not only in his *Confessions* but in his politics, too. So there is a love story and a deconstruction between us.[17]

Derrida makes reference to his work *Circumfession*, its title a deliberate play on Augustine's *Confessions*.[18] In the 'love story' he is much taken by Augustine's prayers and tears, in the 'deconstruction' the relationship becomes much more elusive and idiosyncratic. The reader of this difficult work is forced to question what is indeed meant by 'confession', by 'conversion', by the very name 'God' as Derrida makes known that he is confessing his conversion to an atheist God (*Circumfession* 216, see *Prayers and Tears*, 286). Derrida is acutely cognizant of his Jewishness, though equally aware of his 'broken covenant' with the God of Israel. In that sense he appears most at home with the 'lost Augustine' of the early books of the *Confessions*: 'I became to myself a region of need' (*conf.* 2. 10.18); 'I became my own great question' (4.4.9).

> . . . the omnipresence to me of what I call God in my absolved, absolutely private language being neither that of an eyewitness nor that of a voice doing anything other than talking to me without saying anything, nor a transcendent law. (*Circumfession*, 154)[19]

While it is clear that Augustine's *Confessions* attempt to give voice to a remarkable but elusive divine–human conversation, Derrida conversation is elusive in a different way. It 'goes nowhere and does nothing'[20] is how one commentator describes it. Derrida, in that sense, suggests much that is emblematic about the contemporary state of the postmodern self: divided, unanalysable, solitary, talking to a God who cannot respond – all of this is reflected in the narrative of *Circumfession*. Nonetheless, the dialogue that unfolds is provocatively searching and even mystically open-ended as Derrida questions and deconstructs notions of identity, truth and God, certainly concerns he shares with Augustine. Perhaps, in the end, what is most remarkable about Derrida's and other postmodernist conversations with Augustine is that they are taking place at all.[21]

While these concerns may all seem far removed from what many traditionally understand by spirituality, these contemporary encounters with Augustine highlight how the tradition associated with him is marked by a studied seeking and a thinking searching: disciplined, even provocative inquiry is a vital component of Augustinian spirituality. Contemporary postmodernism, with its fascination with the self, is thus not surprisingly captivated by Augustine's own provocative self-inquiry – but this is also its ambivalence. It is not just any 'inquiry' nor any 'self' that Augustine is trying to model: it is the critical yet humble self, open and searching before the God who does not remain silent. In that sense Derrida and a goodly number of his fellow postmodernist seekers can seem to be distant strangers to Augustine the pilgrim, one certainly engaged in deep conversation, often philosophical, but confident in faith that beyond the conversation there *is* actual encounter, one that leads the self into God – and this encounter has already begun to unfold.

> He showed them where he was staying; they came and were with him. What a happy day they spent, what a happy night! Who is there who can say to us what they *learned* [italics mine] from the Lord? Let us also build and prepare in our heart a house where he may enter in and *teach* us and *converse* with us. (*Io. eu. tr.* 7.9.3)

The teaching, learning, and conversing that is so much a part of Augustine and his spirituality includes but moves beyond the philosophical questions to the divine invitation to intimacy. Without doubt Augustine would continue to insist now as he did then to his philosophical conversationalists that the true philosopher is above all else a lover of God – *verus philosophus est amator Dei* (*civ.* 8.1).

AUGUSTINE 'REDISCOVERED': LATE-TWENTIETH-CENTURY AUGUSTINIANISM

The last decades of the twentieth century have been marked by a resurgence of interest in Augustine, the man and his writings, prompting a fresh look at the spiritual tradition that bears his name. Augustine is the most-cited patristic source in the documents of the Second Vatican Council, an example of this Council's call not only to engage in a serious conversation with the modern world but to do so by returning to the church's deepest and richest tradition. This call had a special impact on those religious communities that followed the Augustinian *Rule*, prompting a renewed interest and study of Augustinian monasticism. The already cited work of Verheijen heralded a new era of studies in pursuit of the *Rule*'s message and spirituality as a model for holiness. In 1967 Peter Brown published his *Augustine: A Biography*, a work which has been translated into a score of modern languages and is emblematic of the renewed attention to Augustine and the world out of which he came.[22] Brown's approach was that of the social historian and so his study signalled that it was no longer simply the theologians or the philosophers who were interested in Augustine. In turn, Brown's work stimulated a host of original studies that are still ongoing, a continued source of challenge and rethinking of the figure and thought of Augustine.

While these studies were under way, the scholarly world was surprised by the announcement that lost texts of Augustine had been uncovered. In 1981 Johannes Divjak published a critical edition of twenty-nine newly discovered letters he had come across while doing manuscript research. It was a stunning event since it revealed hitherto unknown aspects of Augustine and his world: contact with his Greek-speaking episcopal colleagues in Alexandria and Constantinople, alarm regarding the social ills plaguing Roman Africa, turmoil because of wayward clergy. Beginning in 1989 François Dolbeau began publishing a series of newly discovered sermons by Augustine. Some completed partial texts already available, others were totally new. One striking revelation was of a resurgent paganism that prompted an aggressive preaching campaign on the part of Augustine. Suddenly there were new texts of Augustine available which could shed fresh light on the man and his thought. These discoveries also served to reawaken scholarship to the 'other Augustine', the pastor, the spiritual guide, the shepherd of his flock. It became increasingly clear that Augustine could not be accurately known nor understood apart from his sermons and pastoral writing. He was not only nor simply a theologian; in fact, above all else, he was a pastor wholeheartedly involved in the spiritual lives of his faithful. Peter Brown takes note of this in two essays added to his recently reissued biography. He acknowledges that the 'pessimistic' Augustine that emerged as the final product of his erudite work resulted from his almost total bypassing of Augustine the pastor and preacher.

Much of this late-twentieth-century Augustinian scholarship moves beyond centuries of skewed readings marred by polemics and partisanship. The pioneering work of a host of patristic and Augustinian scholars, some of them named in the pages of this study, paved the way for this. Their rigorous labours enabled a more realistic as well as a more holistic rereading of Augustine (as well as all his patristic peers) and signalled a spiritual revival that is still only in its infancy – a new search for an authentic Augustinian spirituality based upon a renewed critical study of Augustine himself and the intentions behind his thought. This new perspective has certainly not put an end to controversy and debate regarding Augustine's role in the development of Western Christianity. This remains particularly true regarding Augustine's perceived impact on a whole variety of contemporary concerns that are seen today as critically important for essential dimensions of an integral spirituality.[23] The very volume of attention being paid to Augustine today offers a unique challenge to hold together and keep in conversation all the differing and often conflicting concerns, methods and approaches Augustine is subjected to today. What is most essential in facing the abundant new readings of Augustine is to keep these readings in conversation with one another as well as with Augustine's own rich complexity: Augustine the God-seeker, Augustine who 'put on Christ', Augustine the monk and pastor, Augustine the thinker, Augustine whose life was nourished by prayer and evangelical love, Augustine the historical figure, living in a real world with all of its blindness and all of its insight. Any spirituality that claims the name 'Augustinian' faces the challenge and responsibility to take into account the 'whole' Augustine, joining him on that same journey that was closest to his own heart.

> You're not yet home (*in patria*), you're still on the way (*in via*) . . . Where are we going? To Christ. How do we get there? Through Christ (*Quo imus*? *Ad Christum*. *Qua imus*? *Per Christum*). (*en*. *Ps*. 123.2)

CONCLUSION: THE END WITHOUT END: THE STILL RESTLESS HEART

Perhaps by now the reader will appreciate the rich complexity of the Augustinian spiritual tradition. Because of the nature and volume of his writings, the deep general impact they had in shaping Western Christianity, the many divergent readings of Augustine that triggered great moments of reform and renewal, it is no small task to make one's way through the density of the tradition to come to what is most central and foundational. Augustine, for sure, that man of restless heart, remains a thinker who does not succumb readily to the normal boundaries of system and synthesis. Thus the heart of his spiritual vision has been perceived in vastly different ways – a fact that this tracing of the Augustinian tradition unmistakably evidences. I have proposed that, despite the apparent complexity of Augustine's writings, his spirituality is centred around a cluster of core evangelical values, all vitally connected with his 'putting on Christ' that marked the real beginning of his spiritual journey: grace, interiority, love, humility and community. It was indeed Augustine's own intimate and transformative encounter with Christ, nourished by the Scriptures and celebrated at Eucharist, that fired and nourished that journey and led him to plumb the depths of those values, now laid before us in volume after volume of his writings. Within those pages we encounter his remarkable and penetrating mind, put to the service of faith, turning critical thinking into a spiritual tool and practice.

What I have just briefly outlined not only explains the dense and divergent history that is the Augustinian spiritual tradition, it also provides criteria for evaluating the claims of those who claim to be or are identified with it. Augustine's spirituality has Christ at its centre; it is broad and sweeping in its concerns; it is imbued with a personalism that defuses its rigour and a sense of community that challenges all individualism; it is ever dynamic in its searching, yet ever securely anchored in God as Truth. To claim to be Augustinian is to strive to be true to all these values; any partial retrieval misses the real Augustine.

What is the future of Augustinian spirituality? An answer is suggested not only by the breadth and depth of Augustine's spiritual vision but also by the critical engagement that vision has generated in contemporary thinking. But that could simply consign the Bishop of Hippo to academics and libraries. As we have seen, Augustine was not simply a thinker and scholar, not simply a theologian or philosopher: he loved God, he relished friendship, he was amazed at the mysterious possibility of a divine–human covenant, he marvelled at the wonders of creation, he never ceased to be astonished by the depth and complexity of the human heart, he anguished over the mystery of evil and human pride and selfishness, he was dismayed at human capacity for self-deception and lust for power. This perspective was the driving force of his preaching, writing and exhortation, done in a way that can still strike present-day readers as incredibly modern and disturbingly threatening. It is both his concerns and his unique way of voicing those concerns that, I would suggest, will keep Augustinian spirituality vibrant, remarkably relevant, and sometimes even controversial. But even when he was most controversial he still had only one aim:

> What do I want? What do I desire? What do I burn for? Why am I sitting here? Why do I live? There's only one reason: so that we may live together with Christ. This is my intense desire, this my honor, this my richness, this my joy, this my glory . . . I DO NOT WANT TO BE SAVED

WITHOUT YOU – *quid autem volo? Quid desidero? Quid cupio? Quare hic sedeo? Quare vivo? Nisi hac intentione, ut cum Christo simul vivamus. Cupiditas mea ista est, honor meus iste est, possessio mea ista est, gaudium meum hoc est, gloria mea ista est . . . NOLO SALVUS ESSE SINE VOBIS.* (*s.* 17.2)

NOTES

CHAPTER 1: THE JOURNEY: AUGUSTINE'S SPIRITUAL VISION

1. There are many fine English editions of Augustine's *Confessions*. For this study I have consulted Sheed's (Sheed & Ward, 1942), Chadwick's (Oxford, 1991), and Boulding's (WSA, 1997), often modifying their translations.
2. Walter J. Ong, *Orality and Literacy: The Technologizing of the Word* (New York: Methuen, 1982), pp. 37ff.
3. Scholars often speak of a thematic rather than a terminological consistency in Augustine.
4. The literature on Plotinus is extensive; see Anne-Marie Bowery, 'Plotinus, *The Enneads*', *AugAges*, pp. 654–7.
5. Pss. 119 (118, LXX) to 133 (132, LXX). Augustine and the Latin West followed the Septuagint enumeration of the psalms. When referring to Augustine's psalm commentaries I will follow his numbering.
6. As recounted by Possidius in his *Vita Augustini*, see *The Life of Saint Augustine by Possidius, Bishop of Calama*, introduction and notes by Cardinal Michele Pellegrino, ed. John E. Rotelle OSA, The Augustinian Series, vol. 1 (Villanova, PA: Augustinian Press, 1988), 12.1, p. 61, also 9.4, p. 55.
7. The word 'spirituality' was never used by Augustine. It was just beginning to enter into the Latin vocabulary in Late Antiquity and only centuries later does it take on its contemporary meaning. Seeking to be true to Augustine, the notion of the 'spiritual journey' captures what in Augustinian terms could be considered the equivalent of a holistic Christian spirituality, one with rich doctrinal content and an explicit commitment to 'living', i.e., making the journey.
8. The quotation marks call attention to the fact that scholarship has interpreted and continues to interpret Augustine's conversion according to a wide spectrum of opposing analyses that range from a purely philosophical conversion to Neoplatonism to a body-fleeing Puritanism.
9. This is not to claim that once this is appreciated someone ought necessarily to agree with how Augustine applies this principle, but it

does demand that the critical reader will need to understand where he is starting from and why – what Augustine's intention was.

10. The literature on this question is extensive, though little of it is in English. See William Mallard, 'Jesus Christ', *AugAges*, pp. 463–70, and Brian E. Daley SJ, 'Christology', *AugAges*, pp. 164–9.
11. Hubertus Drobner, 'Studying Augustine: An Overview of Recent Research' in *Augustine and His Critics*, ed. Robert Dodaro and George Lawless (London: Routledge, 2000), p. 29.
12. A reminder that in ancient Christianity 'holiness' was inconceivable apart from 'orthodoxy'.
13. See, e.g., *s*. 293.7–8.
14. Goulven Madec, the renowned French scholar of Augustine, uses this as the title for his insightful study on Augustine and Christ, *La Patrie et la Voie, Le Christ dans la vie et la pensée de Saint Augustin* (Paris: Desclée, 1989). Augustine's emphasis on the 'Christ Journey' must also be appreciated in the light of its antithesis. There is another journey, that of pride!
15. See Michel Barnes, 'Rereading Augustine on the Trinity', *The Trinity* (Oxford: Oxford University Press, 1999), p. 168.
16. See *Conf.* 6.4.6: 'But just as it commonly happens that a person who has experienced a bad physician is afraid of entrusting himself to a good one, so it was with the health of my soul. While it could not be healed except by believing, I was refusing to be healed for fear of believing what is false. I resisted your healing hands, though you have prepared the medicines of faith, have applied them to the sicknesses of the world, and have given them such power.'
17. It occurs some 430 times throughout Augustine's writings.
18. Gerhard Lohfink, 'The Heritage of Augustine' in his *Jesus and Community: The Social Dimension of Christian Faith*, trans. John P. Galvin (Philadelphia: Fortress Press, 1984), pp. 181–5.

CHAPTER 2: THE GLUE OF LOVE: A 'RULE' FOR COMMUNITY

1. See the volume in this series by Columba Stewart OSB on the Benedictine tradition.
2. George P. Lawless, *Augustine of Hippo and His Monastic Rule* (Oxford: Clarendon Press, 1990), p. 65. See Luc Verheijen, *La Règle de Saint Augustin* (Paris: Études Augustiniennes, 1967).
3. It is often surprising but certainly unfortunate to find modern scholars of Augustine's thought often simply repeating ancient theories regarding his *Rule*. In the sixteenth century Erasmus concluded it must have been written for women because at the end Augustine makes a reference to 'perfume' (he is citing 2 Cor. 2:15, 'giving forth the good odour of Christ') and proposes the document be used as a 'mirror' (*speculum* in the Latin, 'that you may see yourselves in this little book *as in a mirror*': see 1 Cor. 13:12). Erasmus unfortunately

concluded that both 'perfume' and 'mirror' must refer to women, perhaps suggesting that Paul in writing to the Corinthians was only addressing women and seemingly unaware how often Augustine uses both Pauline images throughout his preaching and writing. Erasmus's conclusions were taken up and passed on by subsequent commentators, Bellarmine in particular, and are still repeated today.

4. I have adapted the translation of Robert P. Russell OSA, *The Rule of Our Holy Father St Augustine, Bishop of Hippo* (Villanova, PA: Province of St Thomas of Villanova, 1976). Chapter and paragraph numbers will follow the Russell translation.
5. Tarcisius J. van Bavel, 'The Evangelical Inspiration of the Rule of Saint Augustine', *The Downside Review* 93 (1975), pp. 83–99, hereafter 'van Bavel'.
6. Fr Verheijen comments on Augustine's ideal of the apostolic community described in Acts: '. . . for Saint Augustine the unity of souls and hearts is ecclesial fraternity, first on the long way to God, and then in its definitive accomplishment in the total risen Christ. And although it is embodied in the concrete Church, and more precisely in a monastery or in a home, it is above all a movement tending toward God, a movement *in Deum*. But it is far from being a blind movement. Saint Augustine's concept of Christian and monastic life has a strong contemplative dimension.' Luc Verheijen, *Saint Augustine's Monasticism in the Light of Acts 4.32–35*, the Saint Augustine Lecture 1975 (Villanova: Villanova University Press, 1979), p. 97.
7. Although '*in Deum*' could be literally translated 'in God', its Latin grammatical structure ('*in*' with the accusative designates motion, 'into God') conveys dynamism and movement. It could be rendered 'towards God', 'seeking God', 'into God', 'on the way to God', denoting in the final analysis a vital and vibrant God-directed life.
8. Augustine's preferred term for what we would call 'monks'.
9. See *Praeceptum* V.36. The Roman public bath was not only a place to cleanse the body but a sport, shopping, recreational and conference centre all in one. It could, in that sense, be a place of great temptation. Augustine does not prohibit the servants of God from going to the baths but certainly wishes them to be 'safe' there.
10. See my 'Abundant Supply of Discourse: Augustine and the Rhetoric of Monasticism', *The Downside Review* 402 (1998), pp. 7–25.
11. This comes across most vividly in Augustine's preaching where the congregation responds repeatedly with applause, groans, chest beating, or even distracting noise.
12. There are 93 references to the Pauline corpus, 34 references to Wisdom literature, 19 references to Matthew, 17 references to the Pentateuch, 15 references to 1 and 2 Peter, 14 references to the Prophets, 10 references combined to Luke and Mark, 7 references each to the Psalms, Acts and James, 4 references to the Book of Job, 3 references to the Johannine corpus.

13. George P. Lawless, 'The Enduring Values of the Rule of Saint Augustine', *Angelicum* 59 (1982), pp. 59–78.

CHAPTER 3: TO TEACH BY WORD AND EXAMPLE: CANONICAL SPIRITUALITY AND THE APOSTOLIC LIFE

1. *Life*, 31.6, pp. 129–30.
2. Bernard McGinn, *Christian Spirituality: Origins to the Twelfth Century*, ed. Bernard McGinn, John Meyendorff and Jean Leclercq (New York: Crossroad Publishing Company, 1985), p. 321; hereafter '*Christian Spirituality*'.
3. M.-H. Vicaire, *The Apostolic Life* (Chicago: The Priory Press, 1966), pp. 79–80.
4. See her *Docere verbo et exemplo: An Aspect of Twelfth-Century Spirituality* (Missoula, MT: Scholars Press, 1979).
5. See Grover Zinn, 'The Regular Canons' in *Christian Spirituality*, p. 220.
6. See *Hugh of Saint Victor: Selected Spiritual Writings*, trans. by a Religious of CSMV, with an introduction by Aelred Squire OP, p. 47; hereafter '*Spiritual Writings*'.
7. On the importance of this theme in Augustine see Carol Harrison, *Augustine: Christian Truth and Fractured Humanity* (Oxford: Oxford University Press, 2000), p. 97.
8. Bernard McGinn, *The Growth of Mysticism: Gregory the Great through the 12th Century*, Vol. II of *The Presence of God: A History of Western Christian Mysticism* (New York: Crossroad Publishing Company, 1996), p. 418.
9. Karlfried Froelich, 'Victorines', *AugAges*, p. 868.
10. Richard of St Victor, 'The Mystical Ark' in *Richard of St Victor: The Twelve Patriarchs, The Mystical Ark, Book Three of The Trinity*, Classics of Western Spirituality, trans. and introd. Grover A. Zinn, preface Jean Châtillon (New York: Paulist Press, 1979), p. 45; hereafter '*Richard of St Victor*'.
11. See *Docere et verbo et exemplo*, pp. 205–6.
12. *Expositio in Regulam Beati Augustini*, PG 176, 881–924; hereafter '*Exposition*'. Translations are my own.
13. Zinn, 'Introduction' in *Richard of St Victor*, p. 3.
14. Robert D. Crouse, 'A Twelfth Century Augustinian: Honorius Augustodunensis' in *Congresso Internazionale su S. Agostino nel XVI Centenario della Conversione, Roma, 15–20 settembre 1986*, 3 vols, Studia Ephemeridis 'Augustinianum', 1987), III, p. 167.
15. Robert D. Crouse, 'What is Augustinian in Twelfth-Century Mysticism?' in *Augustine: Mystic and Mystagogue*, ed. Frederick Van Fleteren, Joseph C. Schnaubelt OSA and Joseph Reino, Collectanea Augustiniana (New York: Peter Lang, 1994), p. 401.
16. Ibid.

17. *Semina rationum* is a term used by Crouse to describe such 'sourcing'; see 'A Twelfth Century Augustinian', p. 404.

CHAPTER 4: EXEMPLAR AND RULE OF ALL OUR ACTIONS: AUGUSTINE AND THE HERMITS

1. Popularly called in medieval England the Austin Friars and in France the Grand-Augustins.
2. Jordan of Saxony, *The Life of the Brethren, Liber Vitasfratrum*, trans. Gerard Deighan, foreword and introduction Karl A. Gersbach OSA, ed. John E. Rotelle OSA, The Augustinian Series, vol. 14 (Villanova, PA: The Augustinian Press, 1993); hereafter '*Life of the Brethren*'. I have adapted the text.
3. See the volumes in this series on the Franciscan and Dominican traditions.
4. See the volume in this series on the Benedictine tradition.
5. For this and what follows see Balbino Rano, 'The Order of Saint Augustine: Its Origin and Charism', *Augustinian Heritage* [formerly *Tagastan*] 38/2 (1992), pp. 203–39; hereafter 'Origin and Charism'; Balbino Rano, *Augustinian Origins, Charism and Spirituality*, The Augustinian Series, vol. 3, ed. John E. Rotelle OSA (Villanova, PA: The Augustinian Press, 1994); hereafter '*Augustinian Origins*'. For a particularly English episode in the 'hermit controversies', see Benedict Hackett OSA, 'Geoffrey Hardeby's *Quaestio* on S. Augustine as Founder of the Order of the Friars Hermits' in *Traditio Augustiniana: Studien über Augustinus und seine Rezeption, Festgabe für Willigis Eckermann* OSA *zum 60. Geburtstag*, ed. Adolar Zumkeller OSA and Achim Krümmel OSA (Würzburg: Augustinus-Verlag, 1994), pp. 525–56.
6. The Carmelites were also challenged in this regard.
7. 'The question was not whether one accepted or rejected Augustine, but how Augustine was to be interpreted.' Eric Leland Saak, 'The Reception of Augustine in the Later Middle Ages' in *The Reception of the Church Fathers in the West: From the Carolingians to the Maurists*, ed. Irena Backus, 2 vols (Leiden: E. J. Brill, 1997), p. 372; hereafter 'Augustine in the Later Middle Ages'.
8. Associated with the concept 'school' is what Saak labels a 'quagmire of concepts and terms'. He notes Courtenay's helpful distinction of three concurrent but distinct realities: the Augustinian School (associated with the Augustinian Hermits), Doctrinal Augustinianism (the 'renaissance' of Augustine's thought and its elaboration into theology, philosophy and political theory) and, finally, 'knowledge and use of Augustine's works'. Each of these is a particular reception of the 'original Augustine'. See Saak, pp. 374–5. The notion of an 'Augustinian School' continues to be historically important because of

the questions it raises concerning the possible relationship between such a 'school' and the Protestant Reformation. See Saak, p. 373.

9. *Las Primitivas Constituciones de los agustinos*: (Ratisbonenses del años 1290), introducción, texto y adaptación romanceada para las religiosas, por Ignacio Arámburu Cendoya OSA (Valladolid: Archivo Agustiniano, 1966).
10. Adolar Zumkeller OSA, *Theology and History of the Augustinian School in the Middle Ages*, the Augustinian Series, vol. 6, ed. John E. Rotelle OSA (Villanova, PA: The Augustinian Press, 1996), p. 13; hereafter 'Zumkeller'.
11. The Augustinian Simon of Cascia's (d. 1348), *The Deeds of Our Savior the Lord Jesus Christ* saw wide circulation throughout the Middle Ages.
12. Sharing close ties with the Order of St Augustine (OSA) are those Roman Catholic communities such as the Recollect Augustinians (OAR), the Discalced Augustinians (OAD), the Augustinians of the Assumption (AA) and many contemplative and active sisters' communities who trace their origins or spirituality to the Augustinian Hermits. In the later nineteenth and early twentieth centuries monasticism was revived in the Anglican Church, a number of communities adopting the Augustinian Rule.

CHAPTER 5: A THEOLOGICAL LIFE: A SPIRITUALITY FOR REFORMERS

1. '*Si uis ualde Augustinianus uideri, studium ac uitam illius imitare. Si uiueret Augustinus, citius cognosceret me quam multos, qui titulo illius stultissime gloriantur.*' *Opus Epistolarum*, ed. P. S. Allen et al., vol. 3, no. 899, p. 440. Cited by Nikolaus Staubach in 'Importance of the Fathers for Devotio Moderna' in *The Reception of the Church Fathers in the West: From the Carolingians to the Maurists*, I. p. 455.
2. A helpful introduction for the spiritualities of this period is to be found in John W. O'Malley's 'Reformation and Catholic Reformation Spiritualities' in *The New Dictionary of Catholic Spirituality*, ed. Michael Downey (Collegeville, MN: The Liturgical Press, 1993), pp. 809–17.
3. Charles Béné, 'Érasme et saint Augustin', in *Atti del Congresso Internazionale su S. Agostino nel XVI Centenario della Conversione, Roma, 15–20 settembre 1986*. Studia Ephemeridis 'Augustinianum', 3 vols (Rome: Istituto Patristico Augustinianum, 1987), vol. 3, p. 229; hereafter 'Béné, 1986'. His study of Erasmus and Augustine remains the most important analysis to date, *Érasme et Saint Augustin ou Influence de Saint Augustin sur l'Humanisme d'Érasme* (Genève: Librairie Droz, 1969); hereafter 'Béné, 1969'.
4. Peter Iver Kaufman, *Augustinian Piety and Catholic Reform: Augus-*

tine, Colet, and Erasmus (Macon, GA: Mercer University Press, 1982), p. 114, hereafter 'Kaufman'.

5. Manfred Schulze, 'Martin Luther and the Church Fathers' in *The Reception of the Church Fathers in the West: From the Carolingians to the Maurists*, p. 585, hereafter 'Schulze'. Regarding references to Luther, WA = *Luthers Werke. Kritische Gesamtausgabe.* [*Schriften*], Weimar, 1883ff.; WATR = *Luthers Werke, Kritische Gesamtausgabe, Tischreden*, Weimar, 1912–21.
6. '*Principio Augustinum vorabam, non legebam, sed da mir in Paulo die thur auffgieng, das ich wuste, was iustificatio fidei ward, da ward es aus mit ihm.*' Quoted by Scott Hendrix, 'Luther's Loyalties and the Augustinian Order' in *Augustine, the Harvest, and Theology (1300–1650): Essays Dedicated to Heiko Augustinus Oberman in Honor of his Sixtieth Birthday*, ed. Kenneth Hagen (Leiden: E. J. Brill, 1990), p. 237; hereafter 'Hendrix'.
7. Augustine himself repeats this often: '*simul audiamus* – don't listen to me, let us listen to the scriptures together'; see, e.g., *Io. eu. tr.* 53.7; *en. Pss.* 33.2.16, 119.3, 147.17; *s.* 153.4.
8. '. . . all too often the Reformation is described as the action of a single man, Martin Luther, as the unique spiritual breakthrough to a new era which occurred in a scholar's study. And this action is painted on the backdrop of both a church ossified in its abuses and a fallen, scantily sketched scholasticism.' Lothar Graf Zu Dohna, 'Staupitz and Luther: Continuity and Breakthrough at the Beginning of the Reformation' in *Via Augustini: Augustine in the Later Middle Ages, Renaissance and Reformation, Essays in Honor of Damasus Trapp*, ed. Heiko A. Oberman and Frank A. James, III, in co-operation with Eric Leland Saak (Leiden: E. J. Brill, 1991), p. 117. Regarding 'ungrateful papal jackasses', it is derived from a comment of Luther, WA BR 11.63 (Zu Dohna, p. 121).
9. See Frank A. James, III, 'Gregory of Rimini and Peter Martyr Vermigli' in *Via Augustini*, p. 185; also, 'The Reception of Augustine in the Later Middle Ages', p. 370; David C. Steinmetz, *Luther and Staupitz: An Essay in the Intellectual Origins of the Protestant Reformation*, Duke Monographs in Medieval and Renaissance Studies number 4 (Durham, North Carolina: Duke University Press, 1980).
10. See David Marshall, 'John Calvin', *AugAges*, pp. 116–17, hereafter 'Marshall'.
11. Luchesius Smits, *Saint Augustin dans l'Oeuvre de Jean Calvin*, 2 vols (Assen: Van Gorcum & Co., 1957), p. 271, hereafter 'Smits'.
12. Marshall, p. 119.
13. Joseph Fitzer, 'The Augustinian Roots of Calvin's Eucharistic Thought', *Augustinian Studies* 7 (1976), p. 97.
14. Cited and translated by Fitzer, p. 70.
15. See Francesco C. Cesareo, *A Shepherd in their Midst: The Episcopacy of Girolamo Seripando, 1554–1563*, foreword John C. Olin, The Augu-

stinian Series, vol. 21 (Villanova, PA: Augustinian Press, 1999), pp. 20ff., hereafter 'Cesareo'.

16. Alfredo Marranzini, 'Il problema della giustificazione nell'evoluzione del pensiero di Seripando' in *Geronimo Seripando e la chiesa del suo tempo, nel V centenario della nascita*, Atti del convegno di Salerno, 14–16 ottobre 1994, a cura di Antonio Cestaro (Roma: Edizione di Storia e Letteratura, 1997), p. 243.
17. Cesareo, p. 26.
18. Vittorino Grossi, 'Girolamo Seripando e la scuola agostiniana nel '500' in *Gerolimo Seripando e la chiesa del suo tempo*, pp. 67–8.
19. *Girolamo Seripando, Discorsi: il vescovo, la giustificazione, l'impegno politico*, Quaderni Seripandiani, I, Testo critico e traduzione di Alfredo Marranzini (Rome: Città Nuova, 2001), pp. 110–111, hereafter '*Discorsi*'. The translation is my own.
20. His Registers as Prior General which include some striking letters to the members of the Order struggling to survive in the Rhenish-Schwabian Province show that he had no sympathy for those 'enemies'. See Michele Cassese, 'Girolamo Seripando, il Concilio di Trento e la riforma della Chiesa' in *Gerolimo Seripando e la chiesa del suo tempo*, p. 196.
21. See Vittorino Grossi OSA, 'Seripando, Jerome', trans. A. Fitzgerald OSA *AugAges*, p. 769.
22. Cassese, p. 225.
23. Cited by Gabriele de Rosa, 'Rileggendo le prediche salernitane di G. Seripando' in *Gerolimo Seripando e la chiesa del suo tempo*, pp. 23–4.
24. See David Gutierrez, *The Augustinians from the Protestant Reformation to the Peace of Westphalia, 1518–1648*, History of the Order of St Augustine, Vol. II, trans. John J. Kelly OSA (Villanova, PA: Augustinian Historical Institute, 1979), pp. 61–2, 89.

CHAPTER 6: PILGRIMS TO THE SELF: MODERN AND POSTMODERN AUGUSTINIANS

1. The expression comes from Henri De Lubac, *Augustinianism and Modern Theology*, trans. Lancelot Sheppard, intro. Louis Dupré (New York: Crossroad Publishing Co., 1965, 2000), p. 74.
2. Jean Orcibal, *Jansénius d'Ypres (1585–1638)* (Paris: Études Augustiniennes, 1989), p. 294, hereafter 'Orcibal'.
3. L. Ceyssens, 'Le voies détournées dans l'histoire du Jansénism' in *Jansénius et le Jansénisme dans les Pays-Bas. Mélanges Lucien Ceyssens*, ed. J. van Bavel et M. Schrama, Bibliotheca Ephemeridum Theologicarum Lovaniensium LVI (Leuven: University Press, 1982), p. 11, hereafter 'Ceyssens, 1982'.
4. See Philippe Sellier, *Pascal et Saint Augustin* (Paris: Librairie Armand Colin, 1970).
5. Ewoud M. Mijnlieff, 'The Pursuit of a Phantom or a Disguised Heresy?

Jansenism in the two editions of the *Journal de Trévoux* (1701–1715)' in *L'Augustinisme à l'ancienne faculté de Théologie de Louvain*, sous la direction de M. Lamberigts, avec la collaboration de L. Kenis (Leuven: University Press, 1994), p. 374.

6. See William Doyle, *Jansenism: Catholic Resistance to Authority from the Reformation to the French Revolution*, Studies in European History (London: Macmillan Press, Ltd, 2000).
7. This is brought out clearly in the exhaustive study of Augustine's theology of grace by Pierre-Marie Hombert, *Gloria Gratiae: Se glorifier en Dieu, principe et fine de la théologie augustinienne de la grace*, Collection des Études Augustiniennes, Série Antiquité – 148 (Paris: Institut d'Études Augustiniennes, 1996).
8. Stephen Menn, *Descartes and Augustine* (Cambridge: University Press, 1998), p. 4, hereafter 'Menn'.
9. Gareth B. Matthews, *Thought's Ego in Augustine and Descartes* (Ithaca, NY: Cornell University Press, 1992), pp. 12–13, hereafter 'Matthews'.
10. The question of Augustine and the body is a much discussed topic. See Allan Fitzgerald OSA, 'Body', *AugAges*, pp. 105–7.
11. One need only mention here Charles Taylor and his ground-breaking and likewise controversial study *Sources of the Self*: 'It is hardly an exaggeration to say that it was Augustine who introduced the inwardness of radical reflexivity and bequeathed it to the Western tradition of thought' (Cambridge: Harvard University Press, 1989), p. 131.
12. Henri Gouhier, *Cartésianisme et Augustinisme au XVIIe siècle* (Paris: Librairie Philosophique J. Vrin, 1978).
13. See Michael J. Kerlin, 'Blondel, Maurice', *AugAges*, pp. 103–5.
14. Originally published in French, its English version is found in M. C. D'Arcy SJ et al., *A Monument to Saint Augustine: Essay on Some Aspects of His Thought Written in Commemoration of His 15th Centenary*, pp. 319–53 (London: Sheed & Ward, 1934), hereafter 'Blondel'.
15. '*Ubi enim inveni veritatem, ibi inveni Deum meum*' (10.24.35).
16. *Deconstruction in a Nutshell: A Conversation with Jacques Derrida*, ed. with commentary John D. Caputo (New York: Fordham University Press, 1997), pp. 20–1, hereafter '*Deconstruction in a Nutshell*'. See by the same author, *The Prayers and Tears of Jacques Derrida: Religion without Religion* (Bloomington, IN: Indiana University Press, 1997), esp. Ch. VI 'Confession', pp. 281–329, hereafter '*Prayers and Tears*'.
17. See *Deconstruction in a Nutshell*, pp. 20–1.
18. *Circumfession: Fifty-Nine Periods and Periphrases*, in Geoffrey Bennington and Jacques Derrida, *Jacques Derrida* (Chicago: University of Chicago Press, 1993).
19. See *Prayers and Tears*, p. 288.
20. See Wayne Hankey, 'Re-Christianizing Augustine Postmodern Style: Readings by Jacques Derrida, Robert Dodaro, Jean-Luc Marion,

Rowan Williams, Lewis Ayers and John Milbank', *Animus* 2 (1997), I, no. 23.

21. See, e.g., Jean-François Lyotard, *Confession of Augustine*, trans. Richard Beardsworth (Stanford: Stanford University Press, 2000). For a radically diverse approach see *Radical Orthodoxy*, ed. John Milbank, Catherine Pickstock, Graham Ward (London: Routledge, 1999).
22. Peter Brown, *Augustine: A Biography* (Berkeley: University of California Press, 2000). This is a reissue of Brown's classic work, the original text unchanged, but with the addition of two new essays that take into account scholarship on Augustine since 1967, especially the Divjak and Dolbeau discoveries.
23. For a helpful introduction to this dimension of Augustine see *Augustine and His Critics: Essays in Honour of Gerald Bonner*, ed. Robert Dodaro and George Lawless (London: Routledge, 2002).

FOR FURTHER READING

The Augustinian bibliography is vast. The recent *Augustine through the Ages: An Encyclopedia*, General Editor, Allan D. Fitzgerald OSA (Grand Rapids, MI: William B. Eerdmans Publishing Company, 1999) provides a valuable resource for anyone interested in Augustine, his writings and his impact. There are a host of fine translations of Augustine's works. The ongoing series *The Works of Saint Augustine: A Translation for the 21st Century*, ed. J. E. Rotelle (New York: New City Press, 1990–); *The Fathers of the Church*, ed. R. J. Deferrari (Washington: Catholic University of America Press, 1947–); and *Ancient Christian Writers*, ed. J. Quasten and J. C. Plumpe (Westminster, MD: Newman, 1946–) provide reliable translation and commentary. The journal *Augustinian Studies* (Villanova, PA: Villanova University, 1970–) is devoted entirely to Augustine and the Augustinian tradition. Along with the following suggestions, highlighting books dedicated specifically to St Augustine, readers are encouraged to consult the studies cited in the notes.

Agatha Mary SPB, Sr, *The Rule of Saint Augustine: An Essay in Understanding* (Villanova, PA: Augustinian Press, 1992).

Augustine of Hippo: Selected Writings, trans. and introd. Mary T. Clark, preface by Goulven Madec, Classics of Western Spirituality (New York: Paulist Press, 1984).

Bavel, T. J. van, OSA *Christians in the World: Introduction to the Spirituality of St Augustine* (New York: Catholic Book Publishing Co., 1980).

Bonner, Gerald, *St Augustine of Hippo: Life and Controversies* (Norwich: The Canterbury Press, 1986).

Chadwick, Henry, *Augustine*, Past Masters Series (Oxford: Oxford University Press, 1986).

Clark, Mary T., *Augustine*, Outstanding Christian Thinkers Series (London: Geoffrey Chapman, 1994).

Lancel, Serge, *St Augustine*, trans. Antonia Nevill (London: SCM Press, 2002).

Marrou, Henri, *St Augustine and His Influence Through the Ages*, trans. Patrick Hepburne-Scott, texts of St Augustine trans. Edmund Hill (New York: Harper & Brothers, 1957).

Pellegrino, Michele Cardinal, *Spiritual Journey: Augustine's Reflections on the Christian Life*, foreword Thomas F. Martin OSA, ed. John E. Rotelle OSA (Villanova, PA: Augustinian Press, 1996).

TeSelle, Eugene, *Augustine the Theologian* (New York: Herder & Herder, 1970).

Zumkeller, Adolar OSA, *Augustine's Ideal of the Religious Life*, trans. Edmund Colledge OSA (New York: Fordham University Press, 1986).